Kelly,

We are so happy to have been able to get to know you over this past year and a half. Hopefully you will enjoy getting to know us better through these stories.

May God draw you closer to you as you read your way down this path.

Alan McFall
Sandy

The Pathway to Peace

A Momentary Pause In A Hectic Day

Glenn McCallum and Sandy Letkeman

Copyright © 2016 Glenn McCallum and Sandy Letkeman.

All rights reserved. No part of this book may be used or reproduced by any means, graphic, electronic, or mechanical, including photocopying, recording, taping or by any information storage retrieval system without the written permission of the author except in the case of brief quotations embodied in critical articles and reviews.

WestBow Press books may be ordered through booksellers or by contacting:

WestBow Press
A Division of Thomas Nelson & Zondervan
1663 Liberty Drive
Bloomington, IN 47403
www.westbowpress.com
1 (866) 928-1240

Because of the dynamic nature of the Internet, any web addresses or links contained in this book may have changed since publication and may no longer be valid. The views expressed in this work are solely those of the author and do not necessarily reflect the views of the publisher, and the publisher hereby disclaims any responsibility for them.

Any people depicted in stock imagery provided by Thinkstock are models, and such images are being used for illustrative purposes only. Certain stock imagery © Thinkstock.

ISBN: 978-1-5127-5673-9 (sc)
ISBN: 978-1-5127-5674-6 (hc)
ISBN: 978-1-5127-5672-2 (e)

Library of Congress Control Number: 2016915134

Print information available on the last page.

WestBow Press rev. date: 09/15/2016

Scripture taken from the Holy Bible, NEW INTERNATIONAL VERSION®. Copyright © 1973, 1978, 1984, 2011 by Biblica, Inc. All rights reserved worldwide. Used by permission. NEW INTERNATIONAL VERSION® and NIV® are registered trademarks of Biblica, Inc. Use of either trademark for the offering of goods or services requires the prior written consent of Biblica US, Inc.

Scripture quotations taken from the Holy Bible, New Living Translation, Copyright © 1996, 2004. Used by permission of Tyndale House Publishers, Inc., Wheaton, Illinois 60189. All rights reserved.

Scripture taken from the King James Version of the Bible.

Scripture taken from the New King James Version. Copyright © 1979, 1980, 1982 by Thomas Nelson, Inc. Used by permission. All rights reserved.

Scripture quotations taken from the New American Standard Bible®, Copyright © 1960, 1962, 1963, 1968, 1971, 1972, 1973, 1975, 1977, 1995 by The Lockman Foundation. Used by permission. (www.Lockman.org)

Scripture taken from the Amplified Bible, copyright © 1954, 1958, 1962, 1964, 1965, 1987 by The Lockman Foundation. Used by permission.

All Scripture quotations in this publications are from The Message. Copyright © by Eugene H. Peterson 1993, 1994, 1995, 1996, 2000, 2001, 2002. Used by permission of NavPress Publishing Group.

Contents

Preface xi
Introduction xiii

Begin with a Single Step...1
He Took Our Pain 3
Overwhelmed...6
You Need Other People 10
Be Persistent 13
Worry..15
Never Boring..18
New Beginnings...20
Mercy Reduces Stress 22
Introducing People to Jesus 25
When God Feels Distant..28
When God Works in Our Lives 30
Submission 33
We Are Ambassadors...36
Perspective...39
Goals...42
The Secret to Peace 44
Prayer 48
Christmas...50
Your Potential..52
The Antidote to Stress 55
Connections across Time..57
Take Your Next Step 60
Everything Is Permissible..63

Where Is Your Security?	66
Forgiving Others	68
Selflessness: The Antidote for a Lonely Life	71
Creating Depth	74
Choose Joy	76
New Relationships	78
Be Kind to One Another	81
Peace in the Storms	84
God's Timing	87
Ask for Peace	90
Look Outside Yourself	93
Celebrate Your Freedom	95
You Only Fail When You Stop Trying	98
Where Are You Going?	101
What Do People See?	103
Get Clean	106
Paraphrase	108
A Wise Use of Time	111
Limitless Life	114
Forgiveness	117
Hell on Earth	120
Stuff	123
Sometimes Smart Isn't Smart Enough	126
Good Gifts	129
Plug In and Recharge	132
Where Do You Turn?	135
A Slow Progression in Trust	138
Keep Learning	141
What Is Grace?	144
Are You Sick?	146
What about Him?	150
Live in the Present, Learn from the Past, Plan for the Future	153

Hearing His Voice...157
Keep Your Eyes on the Master..160
Share His Peace with Others 163
Some Parting Words..166

Preface

The devotional studies that you will find in this book were written (some by Glenn, some by Sandy) over the course of two years and distributed to the congregation at Live Oak Church in Flower Mound, Texas. Throughout those two years, many times we received the suggestion that we should edit and publish the devotionals in a single book. At that particular point in our lives, we didn't have the time to do that. Recent events, however, have given us that time, and so we have created the book you now hold in your hands.

Although these devotionals were written years ago, we found as we edited and updated them that the messages they carry remain as current as on the day they were first written. We believe they will bless and entertain you and make you think about some things and show you how you can move toward a more peaceful life. Glenn's dad used to say that peace was best defined as not an absence of troubles but rather a feeling of calm *within* your troubles. That calm comes from a solid understanding that you are loved and valuable. We believe that statement is true of everyone.

It is our hope that this book will provide you with peace (or at least a roadmap on how to obtain it), and that it will cause you to come to a greater understanding of your value and of the joy that is meant to be part of your days on this earth.

Introduction

If you have picked up this book, you find the idea of having peace in your life appealing. This book has been written to help anyone and everyone in what is truly a desire shared by all humanity—a quest for peace. It is written from a Christian perspective because (a) we are Christians and (b) we don't believe you can achieve true peace outside of a relationship with Jesus. Sandy and I love and have prayed for everyone who picks up or looks at this book, and we wish nothing but the best for you. It is our hope that the words between these covers will provide comfort and food for thought and show you the first steps on the path to lasting peace.

Regardless of your background or beliefs, we all live in a world that is characterized by strife and striving. We all feel that pull, that discontent within that impedes our ability to find true peace. This book can help you in that journey, and should that journey include coming into a relationship with Jesus Christ, we will welcome you into the family. If it does not, we hope that you will find peace and wisdom within these pages and that your life will be made better as a result of reading and studying this book.

When reading the pages of this book day by day, you will get the most from it if you (a) only read one per day (after all, the title of this book is not *A Race for Peace*) and (b) spending a little extra time meditating on the quoted scriptures. Now, don't be put off by the word *meditation*; it is just a big word that means "think about." Try this for today: Read John 3:16. Then read it again and substitute your name in place of "the world." Think about the fact that even if you were the only one who needed saving, Jesus still would have died for you. He loves you that much.

I understand that for many of us time is always in short supply (one of the reasons we lead stress-filled lives), so I encourage you that if you don't have fifteen minutes, start with five minutes and just read a devotional each day. Then, time permitting, you can always return to them and dig a little deeper. But if you can set aside just a bit more time (maybe fifteen to twenty minutes) each day for reading, reflection, and study, you can, for that brief moment, put aside the cares of your life and begin your journey along the pathway to peace. However, in whatever manner you approach the devotionals in this book, we wish you well on your journey.

Signpost: Proper fuel propels you forward.

Begin with a Single Step

As long-distance runners know, proper fueling can make or break a race. You can finish strong or run out of gas before you're done. During my eighty-seven-mile bike ride on Saturday, I did not practice proper fueling and I paid the price. I was exhausted and weak at the finish line and didn't feel well for hours afterward. All because I wasn't focused on what I needed to do during the ride to properly hydrate and fuel my body.

Think about what you eat on a daily basis. If you visit the drive-thru more often than your own kitchen, and consider French fries your favorite vegetable, you will not look and feel your best. And it shows!

It's just like that with our spiritual lives. If you don't spend time with God every day, you won't perform up to your potential. You'll lose focus, spend time on things that aren't important or good for you, and you will suffer. However, if you spend time in God's Word every day, offer up your cares and troubles to Him, and live your life focused on Him, you will flourish, living beyond your potential and up to God's potential.

In John 4:10, Jesus talks about providing living water. It is that living water that sustains us, that gives us spiritual life and health. Just as our physical bodies will wither without water, so too our spiritual bodies will wither without the living water that is Jesus living within us. When we are spiritually overflowing with that water, it then flows out from us to others who need that same source for life (John 7:38). When we neglect our physical need for water, we begin to feel a true longing and desire for it. Yet when it comes to the spiritual water, we are quite adept at suppressing that desire. This is dangerous, for without water, without that fuel, we will die.

Proper spiritual fuel comes from only one source, and that is the Word of God. Spending time in the Bible and with Jesus will give us access to that fuel. It is not something that is beyond us. Sometimes people make the excuse that they do not have time (each of us has 168 hours each week, and we make time for things that are important to us). Or they make the excuse that they don't know how (so ask someone) or just feel overwhelmed by stories told by people who speak as if devotional time is not worth doing unless you devote hours and hours to it. No one starts life running. In the same way, our spiritual journey and the fuel that maintains us in that journey can and should start in a manageable fashion.

Stepping-Stones
- Take Stock: Do you feel like you are running on empty?
    - Are you always running from place to place?
    - Are you too tired to properly fuel up?
    - At the end of the day, do you feel further behind than when it started?

- Remedy: For one week, fuel up every morning
    - Spend just five minutes reading the Bible and praying first thing in the morning.

- Practical Advice
    - Tape some scriptures to your bathroom mirror and read them as you get ready in the morning (change them every few days).
    - Replace your bathroom magazines with a Bible.

Signpost: *You are loved more that you can even imagine.*

He Took Our Pain

When Xerox (our cat) was sick and suffering, the idea of having to put her to sleep was killing us. I said to Sandy, "We have to take her pain (on us)." Xerox couldn't help herself. She was suffering and was going to continue to decline and be in even more pain until she died. So to save her from that pain, we had to experience the pain of losing her. We made the decision to put her to sleep.

It was as if the pain needed to be felt by someone—either her or us. There was no option for the pain to just go away. Some of you reading this may understand what we were going through. And some others of you may be thinking, *It's just a cat.* But the pain was real to us. And we took that pain upon ourselves so our little cat wouldn't hurt anymore.

About a week after she died, I realized the spiritual parallel. Before time began, God knew that we (the human race) would be in pain—a pain caused by the weight and torment of our sins. And there would be no way we could get out from under that pain. We would need help. God knew from the moment we were created that He would have to take our pain onto Himself. That was the only way to save us.

That is what Jesus did on a cross almost two thousand years ago. He took our pain and gave us His comfort. He did it willingly and because He loves us. By taking our pain upon Himself, Jesus provided a way for us to be saved. That pain that you feel inside—perhaps a pain that no one even knows about—Jesus has already taken on Himself. He bears your pain, and all you need to do is trust in Him. By accepting and acknowledging that He came to save you, you open the path through which Jesus can give you His comfort.

When you experience pain and suffering in your life, remember that Jesus has already taken that away. He has provided a way out; all you need to do is avail yourself of the path He has made for you. Jesus has said that He is the way, the truth, and the life (John 14:6 NIV). It is through Him that you can find relief from the pain, stress, worry, anxiety, and hopelessness that you may feel each day.

If you have never put your trust in Jesus, I invite you to do so now. He loves you. He took your pain so you could be free. If you have never done so before today, ask Jesus to save you. Acknowledge that He is the pathway to God and that there is no other way. (If you need some guidance on how to do that, turn to the end of the book. It is outlined there.) Once you have done that, you will never be alone. As you make your way through your life's struggles, He will walk with you, guide you, and protect you. You'll still have struggles and problems, but you won't have to deal with them alone.

Jesus is the way. It is through Him that you can find the pathway to peace.

Stepping-Stones
- Have you ever "taken the hit" for someone else? If so, what motivated you?

- Is your view of God more like a cosmic referee or a loving parent?

- Is it a desire to be loved, accepted, or valued that drives you day by day?

- Would peace seem more attainable if you knew you were already loved? (Read John 3:16.) Already accepted? (Read John 1:12.) Valued? (Read Matthew 18:10–14.) Because the truth is, you are.

Signpost: *We lack peace because our focus is wrong.*

Overwhelmed

How am I possibly going to get everything done that I need to? I just need one extra day this week so I can get everything organized! I thought today. When there are too many things going on in my life, I tend to get stressed and overwhelmed, almost to the point of immobility.

I finally convinced my husband to get new carpet for the upstairs. For months I had suggested getting new carpet. It's seventeen years old and is ugly, nasty, builder-quality beige carpet that stains easily (thanks to four hairball-creating cats). He resisted because there was too much clutter upstairs. But then he made the mistake of cleaning up the office, and suddenly it didn't seem so bad. So in a weak moment, he agreed. That was when the stress set in.

We had to remove everything off the floor of the three closets. No big deal, right? Wrong! We had approximately fourteen years of *junk* stored in our closets, almost to the point of overflowing. So for two weeks, we worked diligently to clean and organize, setting things aside for charity, recycling and throwing out other items, and boxing up what we wanted to keep.

Then I got the crazy idea to paint our bedroom since I had gotten new bedding and the paint colors didn't match anymore. And it only made sense that I should paint before the carpet was installed. Add to this, I was making a birthday cake for a friend, making another birthday cake for another friend, had an out-of-town coworker staying with us for a few days, and had family coming to stay in two days. *Yeeha!*

I realized that we had just too much clutter in our home—and too much clutter in my life in general. My desk at work is a mess. I don't feel I can start my day until I get all the nonwork stuff out of my e-mail inbox. Even *those* e-mails stress me out because they are cluttering my work life.

But more than stressing me out, the clutter keeps me from doing the things that are really important: getting to the gym regularly, cooking healthy meals instead of getting takeout or frozen foods from the grocery store, and spending time with God. I got my weekly Bible study done in time, but I didn't spend as much time on it as I should have. I haven't been doing my daily reading regularly. Praying is happening in short snippets throughout the day, but there is no consistency. And I think that might be the reason I am feeling so overwhelmed. I am not putting first things first. I heard a pastor teach that if we are *under*whelmed by Jesus, we will be *over*whelmed by everything else. That has never felt truer than in the last couple of weeks.

It was cathartic to get rid of a bunch of stuff that we hadn't used in ages, and it feels good to donate so much of it to charity. I am determined to get rid of the clutter in my life so I can live with less stress and more freedom. I had no idea how my clutter was dragging me down.

What is cluttering your life? How much stuff do you have that you really don't need? Too many commitments that aren't all necessary? So much clothing (that you don't even wear!) that you can't fit it all in your closet? Closets/attic/garage overflowing with things you just can't part with, even though you don't use or need them? Or do you just spend a lot of time worrying about things that you can't change anyway? Get rid of the clutter in your life, and enjoy the freedom you will experience afterward. And then use the time you previously used to worry about or manage your clutter and spend it with Jesus. In fact, spend it with Jesus first and pray for the strength/time/desire to get rid of the clutter. Matthew 11:28–30 (NIV) says, "Come to me, all you who are weary and burdened, and I will give you rest. Take my yoke upon you and learn from me, for I am gentle and humble in heart, and you will find rest for your souls. For my yoke is easy and my burden is light." I for one really desire a lighter burden.

I am just starting to emerge from my prison of clutter, and it's starting to feel really good. It's like I can breathe again. Thank You, Jesus.

Stuff, clutter, busyness, and noise are all things that interpose between us and things that truly matter. We work long hours to provide for a family that we rarely see because we are at work. We accumulate possessions for the sake of having them and then need a bigger house in which to keep them. We almost never take the time to just be quiet, to be still, to be at peace. "In quietness and trust is your strength" (Isaiah 30:15 NIV). Satan works tirelessly to keep us from being quiet. He works with us (because sadly we rarely resist) to fill our lives to the breaking point just so we won't have time to meet with Jesus.

As a result, the things around us grow in importance while Jesus shrinks in importance. The result of that is a lack of peace in our lives, and like someone who is drowning, we struggle harder to achieve peace rather than simply accept that gift from a loving heavenly Father.

> My peace I give you. I do not give to you as the world gives. Do not let your hearts be troubled and do not be afraid. (John 14:27 NIV)

We need to break the cycle and put Jesus first. As we do so, we will begin to see Him as He really is. And we will begin to be underwhelmed by the world, as we are overwhelmed by Him.

Stepping-Stones

- Do you view your troubles as insurmountable?

- Do you believe that Jesus can't help you (read Jeremiah 32:27) or that He won't (read Proverbs 3:6)?

- Are you able to trust Jesus with the issues of your life? If not, what is is standing in your way?

Signpost: *Life is too hard to go through it alone.*

You Need Other People

On Tuesday night, we had the pleasure of having dinner in Chicago with some old friends and a couple of new friends from South Africa. We are all Christians but come from very different backgrounds: two Canadians, two Americans, two South Africans, three with a Pentecostal background, one messianic Jew, and two who came to Christ as adults. Yet we all had the same God in common, and that in and of itself gave us an ease of conversation unlike anything else. In fact, we spent more than three hours together over dinner, and most of the conversation centered on how God was working in our lives.

It reminded me again of how important it is to have good Christian friends who can edify, encourage, and share God's blessings with one another. We are blessed that most of our friends in Flower Mound are Christian so there is no shortage of people in our lives who are praying for and with us. I can't stress enough how important this is.

Sometimes Christians buy into the idea that they don't need anyone else as long as they have Jesus, and although that is true, it is often spoken with a touch of pride. The idea is that they don't need anyone to help them grow in their Christian walk, rely on, or provide help or assistance. This is where a truth becomes a lie. We have been watching the *Frozen Planet* nature special on Discovery, and one thing we've learned is that it is never good to be separated from the herd. We all have need of other people, and Christians need to spend time with Christians. Our dinner the other night was one of the most uplifting things we have experienced in a while.

Having a loving, supportive pastor and church family are essential in growing your faith and deepening your walk with God. But you cannot beat the camaraderie that comes with spending time with other Christians in a small group setting. You leave events like that with a renewed vigor and determination to be a better Christian, teach others, and reach out to those lonely souls who have never experienced the joy and fellowship that has been so freely given to us through our shared bond with Jesus.

Isolation will never lead to you to peace. Without other people in your life, the inevitable path you will travel is one that leads to bitterness and loss. We need others with whom to share both the good and the bad. The Bible tells us, "Not giving up meeting together ... but encouraging one another" (Hebrews 10:25 NIV). God knows that in addition to helping us grow closer to him, this will simply make our lives better.

I encourage you to join a small group in your church (or find a church) if you are not already in one, and find some Christian friends with whom you can share your joys and sorrows. You will bless them, they will in turn bless you, and most importantly, God will be blessed.

Stepping-Stones
- If you feel alone, first realize that you have value and are worth getting to know.

- Visit churches around you until you find one in which you feel comfortable.

- Spend some time around other people and make time to pray for them.

- Identify three things you can do over the next month to get more involved with other people. Then make a plan to do so.

Signpost: *Don't stop until you get an answer.*

Be Persistent

When I have a lot to accomplish, I make a to-do list so I don't forget anything. I love the satisfaction of crossing items off my list once they have been completed. We all have lists from which we work in our daily lives, but I want to share with you an item I recently crossed off my list—my prayer list, that is.

Our small group created a list of family members and friends who were not saved, and we committed to praying for them. Now, I admit I was not the most consistent pray-er, but I did what I could. And God honored my baby steps. Boy, did He ever. And I am excited to report that Glenn's nephew's new wife accepted Christ on Easter Sunday! We had only been praying for her for a couple of months, and God answered our prayers so quickly! And Christ was front and center at their wedding last week, and there is no doubt these two will have a Christ-centered marriage. God is faithful, awesome, amazing.

I am sharing this to encourage you in your prayer time. Regardless of what you are praying for, remember that God hears all our prayers. We must pray expectantly, in faith, and "boldly approach the throne of grace" (Hebrews 4:16 NLT). Sometimes it is discouraging to pray repeatedly for the same thing and not see results, but remember, everything happens in God's timing and He works everything out to His glory. Don't give up. "Rejoice always, pray continually, give thanks in all circumstances; for this is God's will for you in Christ Jesus" (1 Thessalonians 5:16–18 NIV).

We are explicitly told by Jesus Himself in Luke 11:5–8 and 18:1–8 that we are to persist.

C. S. Lewis stated that he believed that the one side effect of persistent prayer was it showed us what was really important to us. If you've stopped praying, perhaps you should evaluate how important that request was. And if it is important, keep knocking on that door.

Stepping-Stones

- Make a list of your most important and fervent prayers. And expect that you will be crossing things off that list!

- Take some time to think on this question: What have you stopped praying for, and why did you stop? I encourage you to start up again and, in obedience, persist.

Signpost: *It is not your responsibility to fix everything.*

Worry

Twice in the space of about a half hour the other day, I read about why we shouldn't worry. One was in my daily devotional; the other was in my Bible study. The first time I read it, I thought *Hmmm … interesting. Is this meant for me?* (I was worrying about some things … and the more I worried, the worse my thoughts became, and it started to just spiral downward, and it was not going to end well.) After seeing it the second time, I realized God was trying to remind me that He's in control and I'm not. Luke 12 says that God takes care of the raven, who neither sows nor reaps, so how much more will he take care of us?

Worry won't buy you any time. Matthew 6:27 says, "Can any one of you by worrying add a single hour to your life?" (NIV). In fact, it's far more likely to waste an hour in your day! And our days are already so crammed full of activities, do we really have time to spend worrying? Rather, spend a little time in prayer, taking our concerns to God and leaving them in His very capable hands. Everybody worries about all sorts of things, but God knows what we need. All we need to do is seek Him.

Rick Warren stated once that if you are worrying, you cannot be worshipping. The reason for this is that if we are focusing on God, we won't need to worry. But when we focus on ourselves (and our view of our circumstances), we stop worshipping and begin to worry. Look at Peter. When he focused on Christ, he could walk on the water, but when he took his eyes off God, and began to look at his circumstances (from his point of view), he began to sink. The wonderful thing about that account is that when Peter did turn back to God, Jesus reached out and rescued him.

Scripture tells us not to worry about tomorrow because each day has enough problems (Matthew 6:34). I love that scripture because you expect it to say that we shouldn't worry because God's in control (and that is true). But it seems almost sarcastic in the way it finishes by stating that (and I'm paraphrasing now) you have more than enough to worry about today, so why even bring tomorrow into it?

Often we create needless stress in our lives by directing our worry at problems or parts of problems over which we have control. For example, in most cases, we do not worry that we might forget to breathe—something over which we have control and can simply decide to breathe. Rather, we worry about things over which we have absolutely no control. We worry about other people, the economy, or the weather. We waste our time fretting over things we cannot control. So the first thing to do is recognize we are responsible to do whatever we can, but we are not responsible to do things that are beyond us.

So what's the takeaway from this? First, take all your concerns to God and let Him handle them. And when you do that, make sure you leave them in His capable hands. Don't keep taking them back. Second, when you get the same message or scripture more than once, take notice. God's likely trying to tell you something!

And that thing I was worrying about? I prayed and asked God to take care of it, and even though it's not resolved yet, I'm trusting in God to handle it in His way and in His timing. And I've stopped wasting time thinking about it. God's got it. Who better?

Stepping-Stones
- When it comes to issues in your life, it may help to remember that you are expected to do the possible, but the impossible is God's department. Sometimes it can be helpful to spend some time analyzing your worries. (Often they are simply made up or come from your imagining unlikely worst-case scenarios.) It can also be helpful to evaluate the impact if they actually happened. Ask yourself these questions:
    - What is my biggest worry?
    - What would happen if it came true?
    - Is it likely that it will come true?
    - Is there anyone who can help me deal with it?

- Regardless of how you answered the last question, there *is* someone who can help you. God is there for you. Reach out to Him.

- Then get involved in a church. Find that spiritual family that is available to you. There is safety in numbers.

Signpost: Following God's plan for your life is the most exciting journey possible.

Never Boring

All of us have said from time to time, "I'm bored." I'm sure those of you with kids hear it far too often! But I can tell you from experience, life with God should never be boring! A friend of ours said to God just over a year ago that his life wasn't very exciting. Then look what happened: they had to put their beloved cat to sleep, his wife found out she was pregnant, they adopted another cat, their baby arrived weeks ahead of her due date, and now they are selling their house, he has quit his job, and they are moving to Oklahoma to start a new life and an exciting job at Voice of the Martyrs. This all happened in just over a year's time. Life is not boring for them anymore! It's exciting, fulfilling, and maybe even a little scary. But they know beyond a doubt they are walking right in the center of God's will. And He is showing them things and giving them opportunities they never thought possible.

Life should not be boring. It's okay to be content, but it's not okay to settle for less than what God has for you. God doesn't get stuck in a rut. God is not afraid of change. God is not afraid of hard work. He is looking for us to take leaps of faith in His name in order to mature us and to accomplish His work.

Don't let yourself get stuck in a rut in your spiritual life, and don't be afraid to try something new or step outside your comfort zone. Let God out of the box you've put Him in. "Now to Him who is able to do exceedingly abundantly above all that we ask or think, according to the power that works in us, to Him be glory" (Ephesians 3:20–21a NASB). Glorify God by allowing Him to do "exceedingly abundantly" in your life. Experience the true power of God. I promise you, your life will not be boring anymore.

Stepping-Stones

- Are you resisting change in your life? If so, why?

- I was once told that people often mistake the "rims of their rut" for the horizon. You are capable of much more than you think.

- The will of God will not take you where the love of God will not protect you. So if you are bored, spend some time asking God what He has for you to do next.

- Ask yourself: What would I do with my life if I knew I could not fail?

Signpost: Start your day off right.

New Beginnings

First thing tomorrow morning we leave for Winnipeg to attend Glenn's nephew's wedding. On Saturday, he and his fiancée begin a new chapter in their lives—a new beginning. New beginnings are exciting and sometimes a little scary. Going away to college, getting married, having a baby, moving away are all chances to have a new beginning. But new beginnings don't always have to be big.

Every morning, God gives us a new day. Every morning, we wake up and can choose whether to follow God or do our own thing. Every morning, we can choose to be happy that day or choose not to be happy. Every morning, we can choose to spend time with God and grow closer to Him while growing deeper in our faith. No matter how bad today is, no matter how badly we screw it up, we get a do-over tomorrow, and every tomorrow after that. Lamentations 3:22–23 says, "Because of the LORD's great love we are not consumed, for his compassions never fail. They are new every morning; great is your faithfulness" (NIV).

God is faithful to be there, waiting for us every morning, waiting to spend time with us. Tomorrow morning is your first chance for a new beginning with God. No matter where you are in your faith walk, choose a fresh start with God tomorrow. Go a little deeper. Grow a little more. "Taste and see that the LORD is good; blessed is the man who takes refuge in him" (Psalm 34:8 NIV).

As a suggestion, praise is a great way to start your day and set your focus on Jesus. For the next week, start your day praising God, whether you sing a song or simply offer a prayer of thanksgiving. Start each day focused on God, and watch for the difference it will make.

Stepping-Stones
- What can you do to start your day on a positive note?
    - Go to bed earlier.
    - If you like music, perhaps you could play some Christian music as you get ready for the day.
    - Listen to a sermon or uplifting music on your commute.

Signpost: *A judgmental life is an angry, stressful life.*

Mercy Reduces Stress

There is an old saying that states, "Many a word of truth is often spoken in jest." So what does that mean? It means when someone tells you something about him- or herself or about you and then says he or she were "only kidding," you can bet they were trying to tell you something honest. Because you reacted badly, they chose to hide behind the joke.

It's most common to use this approach when you are talking about yourself. I have heard a number of people say, "I don't have the gift of mercy." Then they laugh and usually shrug or slap someone on the shoulder. I shudder when I hear that, and depending on how well I know the person or the mood I am in, I may point out to them that mercy is not just a gift, it is a fruit.

So I did a bit of digging and discovered that mercy is not listed in the main "fruit of the Spirit" passage in Galatians 5:22–23. But I noticed a funny word in the NIV: "But the fruit of the Spirit is love, joy, peace, forbearance, kindness, goodness, faithfulness, gentleness and self-control. Against such things there is no law."

As I read that passage, I got stuck on the word *forbearance*. I know what it means, but I would have a hard time giving a dictionary-type definition. So I looked it up, and I still don't really know what it means. But since I was looking up words, I looked up *mercy*. Look at what I found:

mer·cy—compassionate or kindly forbearance shown toward an offender, an enemy, or other person in one's power; compassion, pity, or benevolence

"Kindly forbearance" … hmmm, those words look familiar, don't they? Something about them not being against the law?

The next time you think that you don't have the gift of mercy, or the gift of self-control, or the gift of love, or you just aren't a gentle person, stop and realize what you are saying. If these fruits are not evident in your life, what is that saying about you and the way you are living?

Jesus tells us in Matthew 7:16 that just as we would identify a plant by the fruit it produces, so too Christians can be identified by the presence of the fruit of the Spirit in their lives. It is frightening how miserably I fail when measured by that yardstick.

So how do we apply this? Well, the next time you are faced with a situation where the fruit you are about to display will not point to God but in fact will point the other way, stop for a moment and ask yourself, "Just whose child am I, anyway?"

It isn't going to be easy, and I imagine that I'll mess it up before I even leave work this afternoon. That will be when I rejoice in the fact that my Father has these gifts in abundance and He "kindly forbears" my failings. Isn't that the least I can do for others? I recall a story Jesus told in Matthew 18:23–35 that gives us a pretty clear picture about how He feels when we don't.

Stepping-Stones
- Are you showing mercy in your life?

- Is there someone in your life that just the very thought of causes you stress?
    - What is the source of that stress?
    - Can you extend mercy to that person? (If you can't, you need to pray for that person.)

Signpost: Prayer opens doors and softens hearts.

Introducing People to Jesus

We attended evangelism training on Sunday morning before church. There we learned some really good ways to broach the subject of Christ with those who are not saved. The step-by-step process to lead others through key scriptures in Romans is practically idiot-proof (with me being the idiot).

So I have everything I need to help others come to Christ, right? Almost. I still have that irrational fear of rejection. I don't want to offend people (and we know that people have found Jesus offensive throughout history (Romans 9:32–33)). But regardless of what I feel, we are commanded to spread the gospel.

I heard a statistic on the radio this morning that over 80 percent of people who accept Christ do so before the age of fifteen. Once you reach adulthood, the percentage drops, and the older you get, the lower the percentage that come to Christ. It is really quite easy to talk to kids about Christ because they have no preconceived notions about Christianity. Each week, these precious children come to Sunday school where we spend time teaching them about God and Christ and showing them how to live like Christ and how to tell their friends about Christ.

We have a captive audience, so to speak, to teach and train and grow in Jesus. But what about our adult friends and family, neighbors and coworkers who are going about their lives with no idea that they need salvation? That's harder, but not impossible. When I was a kid we went to church because that's just what people did on Sunday mornings. But when I grew older, going to church was no longer a priority for me. My attendance dwindled until I was one of the many who just show up at Christmas and Easter. It wasn't until I married Glenn that I found a personal relationship with Jesus.

I encourage you to take evangelism training so you are prepared to lead someone to Christ when the opportunity arises. (I often pray that opportunities fall into my lap so it's obvious to me what I need to do.) I also encourage you to put your beliefs into action and join a group (or start one yourself) that actively tells people about Jesus.

The scriptures tell us that our fight is not with the weapons of this world (2 Corinthians 10:4), but we are certainly in a fight for the lost. Satan doesn't want people to find Jesus, and he has had millennia to hone his skills of deception and twisting the truth and distracting people from the search for Jesus. Everybody searches to fill that God-shaped hole that is inside each of us, and Satan redirects people by getting them to search for other things to fill that hole. All our preparation, training, and efforts are useless unless we are involving God. In order for the veil to be removed from the mind of the nonbeliever, there has to be prayer. I became a Christian because Glenn's family was praying for me, and his family became Christians because a house church on their block was praying for the families on that block. Our job is to work to win souls for the Lord, but the biggest part of that job is prayer. So before, during, and after you are witnessing, remember to pray.

Stepping-Stones
- Is there someone in your life who needs to know Jesus? Pray for them, and don't give up. I would also recommend

reading the book *How to Pray for Lost Loved Ones* by Dutch Sheets.

- Treat them with love and compassion and reflect the love of Jesus into their lives.

- If you are not sure how to share Jesus with people, do some research, talk to your pastor, and read some books on evangelism.

Signpost: *No matter how it may feel to you, God is always close beside you.*

When God Feels Distant

I recently started running again after nursing/resting/rehabbing a nagging injury for six months. In order to start slowly so as not to reinjure the area, I am doing a combination of running and walking. The hardest part about starting over is remembering where you were and thinking you'll never get back there again. I can't even run an entire 5K, yet a year ago, I ran a half marathon. I am starting all over again. It gets discouraging at times, but I keep plugging away. It helps to run with friends since it makes the whole experience that much more enjoyable.

Sometimes we find that we've drifted away from God. Maybe we're a few days or weeks behind in our devotional or Bible reading. Perhaps we skipped the last Bible study because of other commitments, or we find that we've missed more than a few Sunday mornings at church. Regardless of the reason, it's never too late to start over. Deuteronomy 4:29 says, "But if from there you seek the LORD your God, you will find him if you seek him with all your heart and with all your soul" (NIV). So wherever your "there" is, seek God. He is waiting. I like to think that all we need to do is literally turn around (or away from what took us away from Him in the first place) and we could bump into Him because He's so close!

And we don't have to immediately enroll in the next Bible study AND be in worship every Sunday AND catch up on missed devotionals or readings all at once. We can start slowly and progress from there. It's far less daunting if we take it one step at a time. With each step it gets easier. Ask a friend to help keep you accountable. Or even ask a friend to come to a Bible study with you. Before you know it, you're back walking with God daily. And if feels so good!

Start your journey back to God's embrace with this prayer from Psalm 51:10–12 (NIV): "Create in me a pure heart, O God, and renew a steadfast spirit within me. Do not cast me from your presence or take your Holy Spirit from me. Restore to me the joy of your salvation and grant me a willing spirit, to sustain me" (NIV).

Stepping-Stones
- Does God feel distant?
    - He really isn't. He is right there beside you. Take some time to talk with Him and spend time with Him (read your Bible; listen for His direction). Start rebuilding that relationship.

- What is distracting you?
    - If you are spending time with Him, that is wonderful. If you are not, you need to know that He is waiting for you. He has not left you or forsaken you (Deuteronomy 31:8).

- What simple steps can you take in your daily life to feel closer to God?

Signpost: When we trust we are at peace.

When God Works in Our Lives

Who among us, when driving to work or school, loves to see the sign "Road Work Ahead" or "Construction Zone"? Not me. All I think is *Great. They are tearing up the road. It's going to be messy for a while, inconvenient, traffic will be rerouted, and it just takes too long to finish!* We rarely think *This is necessary, and when it's done, it's going to be better than before.*

What about when God's doing some construction in your life? How exciting is that? We should be thrilled. If God is doing a work in our lives, it means He loves us, believes in us, and knows we are ready for the next level in our spiritual walk. The God of the universe is taking an interest in our lives. We should be jumping for joy!

But instead, we often fight it. We resist His urging. We go in another direction. We stubbornly refuse to change. But when we do this, we are only hurting ourselves. God isn't doing this to punish us. He's doing it because He loves us and wants us to be new and improved. Just like roadwork, there comes a time when we need some improvements. The road needs to be expanded for increasing amounts of traffic. We need to expand our minds and hearts to carry out God's plan. The road has dangerous potholes that need to be filled. We have issues or insecurities that need to be fixed so we can better serve Him. When the road is finished, we quickly forget how long it took and how painful the process was. When God is finished working on the current issue, we forget the angst, confusion, and worry and instead praise Him for His work in us and the results of that work.

God is working in my life right now. I am doing my best to submit to His will, but it is hard at times. I'm confused, isolated, and, yes, scared. I am scared to change. I am scared of leaving my comfort zone for something new. Why don't I realize that He has something better for me, and that I just need to trust Him? He is faithful; I know that in my heart. So I'm trying. I'm praying my way through it. I am seeking godly counsel. So far, the changes I've noticed have been great! I give glory to God that He can change someone like me.

So here's my humble suggestion. Trust me, it works. Instead of avoiding the work God wants to do in your life, submit to His will and go with it. Ultimately, He's right. Delay is disobedience.

Stepping-Stones
- Where is God leading you?
  - If it is somewhere that scares you, remember that he is with you (Psalm 23).
  - If you can't see what the future holds, remember your future is His past. He knows what is going to happen, and He will be faithful.

- If you are resistant, ask yourself why.
  - If the answer is that you are afraid, you can fight that with biblical truths:
    - God is trustworthy.
    - God knows more than you do.
    - God loves you.
    - God will never leave you.
  - If the answer is that you are comfortable, you need to realize that the best is yet to come.
    - God has a plan for your life.

- In all aspects of life, improvement requires effort.
- What steps can you take (no matter how small) to begin that improvement?

Signpost: *Submitting to one another builds peaceful relationships.*

Submission

I used to watch wrestling when I was a kid. (I blame my brother for that.) In order for a wrestler to win the match, the other wrestler had to say, "I submit!" So I used to think that submitting was simply giving up. And in that context, I suppose it was.

However, God's definition of submitting is very different. In Ephesians 5:21, Paul says, "Submit to one another out of reverence to Christ" (NIV). Does this mean if a group of people is trying to reach a decision, whoever comes up with an answer first wins? Of course not. It means that in all things you discuss and arrive at a decision together (in marriage, friendship, the church). It's a mutual, humble cooperation with others.

Colossians 3:18 says, "Wives, submit to your husbands, as is fitting to the Lord" (NIV). This doesn't mean that the husband makes all the decisions in the marriage and rules with an iron fist. The goal, especially in marriage, is consensus. However, after much discussion and prayer, if consensus cannot be reached, the husband is *on the hook* for the decision he makes. On the hook— with God. To be honest, I'm happy to be the wife and not have that kind of responsibility! Wives, be thankful that God gave us the role of submitting, and husbands, think carefully about the decisions you make. The counterbalance to that submission is found immediately in verse 19: "Husbands love your wives and do not be harsh with them."

Finally, and most importantly, "Submit yourselves, then, to God" (James 4:7a NIV). Yield to His authority, give Him control of your life, and be willing to follow Him. He's in control anyway, so why fight it?

Submission is rarely easy. It means giving up our desires, control, or will to another. It means not always getting what you want but yielding for a greater good. It is voluntarily cooperating with another out of love and respect for God first and then out of love and respect for that person or persons. But submission is absolutely vital for a healthy marriage, loving and trusting relationships, and to effectively serve Christ.

If you find submitting to others hard, start first with submitting to Christ. He is always faithful and trustworthy and will never let you down. When you do yield to God's will, it's actually quite freeing! And once you're comfortable with that, submitting to others will come naturally out of your love and respect for Christ.

Sadly, this is one of the most often twisted truths in the Bible. It does not mean that the husband always gets his way. The lessons in the Bible are never one-sided. Consider these scriptures in connection with each other: "Submit to one another," "Wives submit to your husbands," "husbands love your wives," and "do not be harsh with her," and in Ephesians 6:4, "Fathers, do not provoke your children to anger" (NLT). All these passages work together to illustrate the truth that a family that is living fully submitted to God will naturally prefer one another in love. And that describes the path to peace in anyone's family.

Stepping-Stones
- Who do you know that practices submission in a positive and effective manner?

- Do you know anyone who uses the concept of submission as a tool to manipulate others?

- Do you have areas in your life where submission (to others or to God) is difficult for you?

- How can you better practice submission?

*Signpost: We are to be in the
world but not of the world.*

We Are Ambassadors

The tagline in one of the commercials for this season's *The Apprentice* is "When celebrities behave badly, everybody wins!" This makes me absolutely crazy! Since when did it become okay to celebrate bad behavior? Teen moms get their own TV show. Stars admitting drug addiction or having affairs get on the cover of *People* magazine. Not to mention all the reality shows on TV, most of which are not based on any normal person's reality and are full of contrived drama!

But then I have to remind myself that this is how the world views life. The world that has no hope and no Savior. As Christians, we are IN the world, but we are not to be OF this world. We are called to a higher standard of behavior. In Ephesians 4:1, Paul writes, "I, therefore, a prisoner of the Lord, beseech you to walk worthy of the calling with which you were called" (NLT).

"Walk worthy of the calling with which you were called." When we accepted Christ, our lives changed forever. We have a new standard, a new goal, to become more and more like Christ every day. But it's even more than that. In 2 Corinthians 5:20, Paul says, "So we are Christ's ambassadors; God is making his appeal through us."

Take a moment and think about that word *ambassador*. What are some of the qualities of an ambassador? Well, first, when they speak, they do not voice their own opinions or thoughts. They speak what they are told to speak; they speak what their king (or government) has commanded them to speak. We have not been given the luxury to speak our own mind; we are to speak the truth (in love, absolutely) that this world with its "reality" and twisted truth so desperately needs to hear.

Second, an ambassador must be ready at any moment to be called home. His or her time at his or her post is decided by the One who gave them that post. Are you ready? Do you live your life in such a manner that you are ready, at any moment, to leave and make a final report of how you handled your ambassadorship?

Third, they are accountable for what they say and do. In the earthly realm, they become that country to the country of their residence. The embassy grounds become the legal soil of the represented government. In a very real sense, an ambassador lives in the country to which he has been sent but is kept apart from it at the same time. He is "in" the country but not "of" the country.

So, just as an ambassador is a representative, authorized, empowered, and commissioned by the ruler who sent him, we are to be representatives of our Father's kingdom. In a world that is so very dark, we are to reflect the light. We have not only been entrusted but also commanded to proclaim the good news of Jesus, and we are to do it in such a way as to bring honor to our king. We are not free to put our spin on the gospel; our opinions are not to be considered in this. The King has given us a job to do, and we are to be doing it every minute of every day.

The saying goes "You might be the only Bible that a person reads." Do you want to be the reason that someone turned from the Lord? Do you want, through your actions or inactions, to be used by Satan to cast our Lord in a bad light? Or do you want to literally shine as an example of the love and joy of Jesus?

We forget sometimes that we must always be on our best behavior, living Christ-centered lives and loving others as Christ loves us. We need to be the example of how living for Christ is far better than a life without Him. And all that is required of us is that we be willing.

In John 13:35, we are told the manner in which we are to act so people will see a difference and a reflection of Christ in us: "By this everyone will know that you are my disciples, if you love one another" (NIV).

Stepping-Stones

- Are you displaying the love of Jesus to the world?

- Is your character one of condemnation or grace?

- Is your life presenting the hope of heaven or the opinions of man?

- We cannot retell a message that we do not know. To be a proper ambassador, we need to spend time with our King.

Signpost: *Gratitude is only possible if you understand how much you have been blessed.*

Perspective

I am coming to the end of five straight weeks of travel, and from my perspective, that's quite a bit of travel. And this story is about exactly that, perspective. On one of the trips, we stayed over the Friday night at the airport hotel in Chicago. During dinner in the hotel restaurant, we were hit between the eyes with a healthy dose of perspective.

While we were eating our dinner, a young family came in with two children, one boy and one girl—your typical, perhaps even stereotypical family. But with one very big exception. The boy had no arms. He had hands, but they came straight out from his shoulder sockets. His wheelchair (I guess there were issues with his legs too) had a little joystick for navigation that was up by his shoulder, which was how he directed the chair. We were struck by how well adjusted not only the boy but also his whole family was to this incredible disability. I sat there and thought to myself, *Suck it up, princess. You have arms.* Perhaps that seems harsh or crude, but it packed a punch to me. I struggle with many things in my life. I have many flaws that I try to fix and fail, I have a business that (praise God) keeps me employed but does not keep me in the manner to which I would like to become accustomed, I have clients that don't sign when I want them to, I have New Year's resolutions I can't keep, and sometimes I really don't like my life. But that night I learned to suck it up because I have ARMS.

It is amazing how a little perspective can provide clarity. Because while I do have my arms (really, when was the last time any of us thought to pray and thank God for our arms?), I still have daily struggles, pressures, and real problems I need to deal with. They are my problems and they are real—from my perspective. It reminds me of the saying (regarding young love), "It may only have been puppy love, but it was real to the puppy." Our problems are real to us and are the things God has given us and we need to deal with them. (And sometimes they are the result of really stupid choices on our part.)

But thinking about the boy with no arms makes me realize that there are certain things, certain everyday things, for which he needs the help of someone else to accomplish. I don't imagine he can get dressed alone. He can't bathe alone. There is much he cannot do alone.

The difference is that he knows he can't do it alone while we delude ourselves into thinking that we can deal with our problems on our own. But we can't. We need help with our problems as much as that little boy needs help getting dressed in the morning.

First Samuel 22:12 says, "The Lord will not forsake His people for His great name's sake, for it has pleased Him to make you a people for Himself" (Amplified Bible). And Genesis 28:15 says, "And behold, I am with you and will keep (watch over you with care, take notice of) you wherever you may go, and I will bring you back to this land; for I will not leave you until I have done all of which I have told you" (AB).

> The LORD is near to all who call on him, to all who call on him in truth. He fulfills the desires of those who fear him; he hears their cry and saves them. (Psalm 145:18–19 NIV)

The Bible tells us we have someone who is willing and able standing by just waiting for us to swallow our pride, turn to Him, admit our need, and ask Him for help. I don't know how people make it through life without the Lord. We are not alone; He will not leave us or forsake us. Our God is "mighty to save." Yes, I thank God for my arms, but more than that, I thank Him that with all the issues and problems and frustrations that I face every day, I don't have to face them alone. And neither do you.

Stepping-Stones
- God puts people in our lives to help us, and equally, He puts us in the lives of others so we can help them. Is it easier for you to ask for help or to help others? Both are necessary.

- Is there someone you need to help? Someone you need to encourage? Don't delay any longer. Reach out to them. Chances are they need you.

- While you are at it, is your pride standing in the way of asking for help? Don't rob others of the blessing of helping you. You don't have to be able to do everything on your own.

***Signpost:** If you don't have a destination, how will you know when you have arrived?*

Goals

Most companies have a mission statement. Our company's, if we were to write it down, would probably be something like "Run the company as lean as possible, stay focused on building the company (even when money is tight), convince our clients we're better off than we are, and be honorable in all our business dealings so we don't need a salesman because potential clients call us for our product." Okay, that might be a bit long, but that's how we've run our company for almost eight years. But if we didn't work hard and believe that things would change for the better, we would never have made it.

The other day, our couple's devotional urged us to write a mission statement for our marriage. It had never occurred to us to do this. So we pondered it for a while and came up with a simple mission statement that reflects how we want to grow emotionally and spiritually. At the end of the year (or maybe sooner), we can review it and see how we're doing.

Do you have a mission statement for your life? For those who are married, do you have a mission statement for your marriage? If you don't, you might find (as we have from time to time) that you're just drifting through life, not really knowing where you are going or how you are doing. If our church didn't have a purpose, we might just show up every week to hear the pastor talk and never do one thing for the kingdom.

I love to set goals. It gives me something to work toward. I can set up a daily/weekly/monthly plan with the steps needed to achieve my goal. I'm biking 150 miles in two days in May. If I didn't have a plan, I wouldn't be able to complete the ride. It's not something you can wake up one day and do. Your life or marriage is the same way. Create a mission statement this week, and set some milestones you hope to achieve along the way. Make sure that God is front and center in your mission. Then see how your plan unfolds in the coming months and years.

Let's take a look at Proverbs 29:18a: "Where there is no vision, the people perish" (KJV).

Now let's go a step further and really study that verse. Let's rewrite it and personalize it to see what it has to say about having vision or goals in our lives.

"When I have no vision (goals) for my life, it becomes meaningless."
"When I have no vision for my relationships, they begin to fail."
"When there is no vision in my church, it begins to stagnate."

Stepping-Stones
- After praying about your life goals and asking God what His goals for your life are, write a mission statements and goals for
    - your relationship with God,
    - your marriage and other relationships,
    - your career,
    - helping others.

- Then develop a plan. Just some simple steps that will help you achieve these goals.

Signpost: *Peace is a product of proper focus.*

The Secret to Peace

There is a song ("Trading My Sorrows" by Matt Redman) with a chorus of "Yes, Lord, Yes, Lord, Yes, Yes, Lord." I realized the other day that the words of that chorus hold the key to contentment, the secret to peace. To realize that in the midst of anything and everything, the answer that leads to peace is "Yes, Lord." The other week, I was reading about Christians in persecution. In one story, a couple's child had been killed for spreading the gospel, but their response to this tragedy was not anger but rather "We are not angry. We are proud that our son died for the sake of Christ." What an amazing statement! Meanwhile, we worry about things like money, clothing, and food when our Father in heaven knows what we need even before we ask (Matthew 6:8).

When our company was starting out years ago, there was little or no money (and I mean NO money). We learned that our provision comes from the Lord, not through man or the works of man. This is a very timely lesson for all of us given the current state of the world economy. Pity the person who has to rely on the economy for his or her provision. Our provision comes from our Father in heaven.

The company has been doing well for a few years now, and although we haven't gotten rich, we certainly aren't starving. (Come to think of it, we didn't starve when we didn't have money either.) But over the last little while, we have been hit with some unexpected expenses and have watched the fruit of our efforts flow out a little bit faster than we wanted. It is so easy to forget the lessons that we learned, so easy to begin to look at our work, job, and efforts as our source of provision. How foolish. With that focus on ourselves, the old feelings of panic resurfaced; feelings (with regard to money) that we thought had long ago been crushed under the weight of the evidence of God's provision in our lives.

God will not allow us to be tested to any limit beyond what we can bear (1 Corinthians 10:13), but I often add my own comment after that: "I think God has too high an opinion of me." We need to remember that in the midst of the chaos that is our lives and our world, we are not of this world (John 15:19) and our provision does not come from this world.

When we learn the truth behind the words "Yes, Lord," we can say with the apostle Paul:

> I have learned to be content whatever the circumstances. I know what it is to be in need, and I know what it is to have plenty. I have learned the secret of being content in any and every situation, whether well fed or hungry, whether living in plenty or in want. I can do all this through him who gives me strength. (Philippians 4:11b–13 NIV)

God provides "according to his riches of His glory in Christ Jesus" (Philippians 4:19 NIV). (It seems to me that Philippians 4 would be a good chapter for the whole world to read right now.) The secret to contentment is to have that truth become real in our lives. Jesus makes it quite clear as he tells us, "Don't be afraid; just believe" (Mark 5:36b NIV). Simple instructions yet not quite so simple to carry out. But they hold the key to a life of peace and contentment as we give up our cares for His love.

The secret to peace and confidence lies in keeping our focus on Jesus. Look at Peter in Matthew 14:31. Panic and failure were the result when he took his eyes off Jesus.

Stepping-Stones
- Our lives are to be lived in partnership with God, so while peace comes from a focus on Jesus, this does not absolve us of our responsibilities for that area. For instance,
    - Finances: If you are worried about your finances, your first question should be: Am I tithing to God's work? And then: Am I being wise with my money?
    - Relationships: Are you treating people the way you want them to treat you?
    - Health: Are you eating right and exercising?
    - Work: Are you doing your best? Arriving on time? Helping others? Are you projecting a positive attitude?
    - Future: Are you doing all you can? You shouldn't worry about things that are beyond your control, but you should work hard on the things that you can control.

- Fill in the blanks below. Indicate where your focus is for each area of your life (1=all on you; 10 = all on Jesus). Then go back and note the level of peace you have regarding each area (1=very anxious; 10=completely at peace).
    - With regard to my finances, I am focusing at a number ___, and my level of peace is ___.
    - With regard to my relationship with my spouse (or GF/BF), I am focusing at a number ___, and my level of peace is ___.
    - With regard to my relationship with my children, I am focusing at a number ___, and my level of peace is ___.

- With regard to my health, I am focusing at a number ____, and my level of peace is ____.
- With regard to my job/schoolwork, I am focusing at a number ____, and my level of peace is ____.
- With regard to my future, I am focusing at a number ____, and my level of peace is ____.

Signpost: *Prayer strengthens our relationship with God.*

Prayer

Today was crazy busy at work. At 9:00 tonight when I finally stopped to take a breath and get ready for bed, I remembered that I had not sent the prayer e-mail yet. And I had nothing. So I prayed as I opened my Bible-reading plan, "God, I need something. Give me something to write about." As soon as I opened my journal to today's date, this scripture jumped out at me: "God has surely listened and heard my prayer" (Psalm 66:19 NIV). Ha! God cracks me up sometimes. I love when I get immediate answers to prayer. It doesn't happen often, so when it does, I take notice!

Prayer is the most powerful weapon we have. How often have you heard people say (or have said yourself), "Well, the least I can do is pray." In fact, prayer is the MOST that you can do! You are appealing to the One who can do anything, amazing, miraculous things. Ephesians 3:20 says, "Now to him who is able to do immeasurably more than all we ask or imagine, according to his power that is at work within us" (NIV). Immeasurably more than all we ask or imagine. Wow. Who wouldn't want to harness that power?

Last night at the ladies dinner, we exchanged prayer requests. Each person has another lady praying for her for an entire month until the next ladies dinner, where we'll do it all over again. It is so neat knowing that someone else is going before God in prayer on my behalf. Now not only am I praying, but a fellow prayer warrior is also pounding on God's chest for me.

I feel privileged to pray for my partner this month, and I can't wait to see what God does for her through my prayers. I encourage you to find a prayer partner and share your prayers with him or her so not just one but two of you can "draw near with confidence to the throne of grace, so that we may receive mercy and find grace to help in time of need" (Hebrews 4:16 NASB). "I will answer them before they even call to me. While they are still talking about their needs, I will go ahead and answer their prayers!" (Isaiah 65:24 NLT).

God is not surprised by our prayers. He knows our needs and could answer them without our involvement. But He wants to build a relationship with us, and to build any relationship, you need to spend time together, communicate, and build trust between you. Prayer (talking) and being quiet (listening, or meditating) is the way we do that with God. This quiet time with just you and God is also one of the pivotal steps in finding peace in your life.

Stepping-Stones
- Identify some time/place where you can devote yourself to prayer. Some suggestions are
    - during your commute,
    - waiting in line (for anything),
    - while brushing your teeth.

- Make prayer a part of your daily life.
    - Set aside a specific time to pray.
    - Also use life's little delays as an opportunity for some quick prayer.

Signpost: *When we turn our focus outward, stress is reduced.*

Christmas

I do not look forward to Christmas. It annoys me that Christmas ads (sorry, *holiday* ads) are on TV before Halloween. I do not enjoy the crowds in the stores. And don't even get me started on the insanity of mall parking lots, the rampant materialism, and the commercials where people give CARS as gifts. Really? In whose world does *that* happen?

And I really hate all the rushing around. My life at Christmas consists of getting on an airplane and flying to a place much colder than Texas. Strike one. Then our days in Canada go something like this: wake up early, squeeze in a workout (to work off all that Christmas baking!), work until lunchtime, meet somebody for lunch, possibly visit somebody else in the afternoon, meet yet another person for dinner, get home late, crash, wake up the next morning, repeat daily. Strike two. Did I mention I have to work while on Christmas "vacation"? Strike three. I could go on, but I'm out.

Okay, let me hop off my soapbox now. Anybody else feel like this? Well, I'll let you in on a little secret I learned a long time ago and have to keep reminding myself every year: IT'S NOT ABOUT YOU!!!! (OR ME!!!)

Christmas should be first and foremost a celebration of the birth of our Lord and Savior, Jesus Christ. Regardless of what advertisers and the media try to shove down our throats, we know the real reason for the season. We should rejoice in that. Once all the presents are opened and the food is consumed, we still have Jesus.

Christmas is also a time when I get to see my entire family, as we all travel home from various places to spend time together. My parents are eighty-five years old, and I won't have many more Christmases with them. Glenn's mom turns eighty-one on Christmas Day. How cool to share her birthday with Jesus? But she's not getting any younger either. Glenn and I get to see friends we grew up with and catch up on one another's lives.

Once it's all said and done, and we are wearily winging our way back to Texas, I never regret all the running around so I could see everybody at least once and hopefully more. In fact, I always wish I had more time. So this Christmas, cherish the time with your family and friends, give more than you receive, share the love of Christ, and thank God for the birth of His Son.

I feel better already. I pray you do too.

Merry Christmas!

Focus makes all the difference, whether it is during times of stress, crisis, or even peace. A focus on others or on the Lord increases the joy in the circumstances.

Stepping-Stones
- Regardless of the time of year, what activities or events in your life cause you stress? What steps can you take to reduce that stress?

- What opportunities exist around you to help others?

- Who in your circle of friends is the most stressed? What can you do to alleviate some of that stress?

Signpost: *God created you for a purpose. Identify it and pursue it.*

Your Potential

My husband jokes that he lives in constant fear that the talent police will show up at his door one day and say, "What do you think you're doing? You don't know how to run a company!"

Do you ever feel that way? That you are masquerading through life as something you're not? We can fall into two camps. Either we're putting on airs and trying to fool people into believing we're something we're not, or we're wondering how on earth we are able to do what we do when we obviously don't have the skills to actually do it!

Glenn was working with another vendor to set up a new client. The other vendor kept putting him off while Glenn was ready to integrate our system with theirs. Then he received an e-mail from their salesman saying, "Rick, I don't know how long I can keep lying to Glenn about our ability to integrate with their software." The salesman meant to send the e-mail to his boss, but for some inexplicable reason, he sent it to Glenn instead. Needless to say, Glenn contacted our mutual client and warned him that this vendor could not deliver what they had promised. They tried to fool the client into believing they could do the job when they obviously could not.

Then there are people who are very talented but don't believe they are. In all likelihood, they are not living up to their potential (either professionally or spiritually) because their insecurity holds them back. And because of this, they are not living the life God has planned for them.

God created you for a reason, and He gave you special and unique talents. He equipped each of us with abilities that He fully expects us to use. Don't let your talent lie idle and don't squander it. Rather, use it for the glory of God and His kingdom. Maybe your talent isn't fully developed yet, but the only way to improve is to use it!

William Shakespeare said, "Be not afraid of greatness: some men are born great, some achieve greatness and some have greatness thrust upon them" (*Twelfth Night* Act 2, Scene 5). God made you to be great. Don't sell Him (or yourself) short. If you serve God with all your abilities and all your heart, you won't need to pretend to be something you're not.

We are given talents and abilities designed to be used for God's purposes. Satan has two ways of stopping that from happening. He can cause you to be too afraid to try, or he can have you redirect those talents for the use and benefit of things other than God's purposes.

Read the parable in Matthew 25:14–29 to see what happens when we don't properly use the resources God has provided. Now let's personalize that lesson. Is your fear (or insecurity) robbing you of achieving your potential? Remember God's promises and use them to fight that fear.

You are not alone. "I will never leave you; never will I forsake you" (Hebrews 13:5 NIV).
You don't need to be afraid. "Perfect love drives out fear" (1 John 4:18 NIV).

Your worth is not tied up in your success. You have worth because God says you are valuable. With God's leading, search out the greatness He has for you and go for it. He's there to catch you if you fall and rejoice with you when you succeed.

Stepping-Stones
- What are you good at?

- What do you like to do?

- What opportunities exist to do these things to help others?

- Is it your mission (will you volunteer?) or your vocation (will you make it your career?)?

Signpost: Gratitude deflects worry.

The Antidote to Stress

It's that time of year again when we eat too much good food and reflect on the things for which we are thankful. So in the spirit of the season, let me give you some "food" for thought.

I am thankful for our financial stress a couple of years ago, when we had much debt and little income, because it taught me to rely on God and not a paycheck.

I am thankful we went through marital troubles that came close to divorce because it taught us both how to be better spouses and that a successful marriage includes a third person: Jesus.

I am thankful that God drags me (sometimes kicking and screaming) out of my comfort zones because it's then that I grow emotionally and spiritually.

I am thankful that God doesn't answer all my prayers with a yes because it means that I must have deeper faith to trust that He knows what's best, even when it hurts.

I am thankful for my church family, who is a great stand-in for my bio-family back in Canada. Doing life with you is truly a blessing and a joy.

And of course I'm thankful for all the good things God has blessed me with. But the trials and tribulations are what grow a person's character and faith.

What are you thankful for today?

So often our thoughts focus inward, and while this makes perfect sense (after all, most of our stimulus comes from our own senses and thoughts), it also traps us inside ourselves. We don't notice things or people around us because we are focused on our own issues. All else is excluded. This is the first step on the path to stress, selfishness, loneliness, and depression.

The antidote is to step outside yourself and your (likely very real) problems. Begin by looking for anything for which you can be grateful and then move on from there. Look for those around you who need help and help them.

It isn't easy to break the cycle, but it can be done. "Don't worry about anything; instead, pray about everything. Tell God what you need, and thank him for all he has done" (Philippians 4:6 NLT).

Stepping-Stones
- What is weighing on your mind today? Can you identify anything related to that about which you can be thankful? (For example, I recently got hit with a large tax bill, and I chose to focus on being grateful that I have a job when so many do not.)

- Recognize that you can't solve every problem and decide to pass the worry over to God.

- Do a word search in the Bible on worry and study the scriptures that you find.

Signpost: *You are loved by the One who knows the beginning and the end.*

Connections across Time

Awhile ago I was in Rome, a city rich in history (both good and bad). The Vatican was stunning, Saint Peter's Basilica was amazing, and the Coliseum and Pantheon were surreal. But the thing that really gave me chills was a road. Not just any road, but a cobblestone road. And not just any cobblestone road, but the Appian Way, a road built over two thousand years ago. That is impressive in and of itself, but did you know that this was the road that Paul and Peter would have walked on when they entered Rome? This was still the original road; nothing about it has changed. And I was walking on the very place where Paul and Peter walked. That's what gave me chills.

Most people who visit Rome spend their time looking at the creations of man. They look in awe at the Coliseum, the churches, the sculptures, and the paintings. Your mind begins to reel under the onslaught of all the culture; there is so much history, and it is so old. You walk through the narrow streets and suddenly turn a corner and find a building that was ancient even before our continent was discovered. It is impossible to visit and not be in awe of what man created so long ago.

And it was man who created that road. The Romans knew how to build roads, and they are still used today more than two thousand years later. The Romans knew a lot of things, and God used that. God picked the precise moment in history to step into time and provide a way of salvation for the helpless race of man. He used those road builders. He used their fear and barbaric forms of execution to sacrifice His Son. Then when His plan was fully realized and Jesus rose and the Holy Spirit empowered the disciples, they used those roads built by the same ones who had crucified Christ to take the gospel to the known world.

The works of man are impressive, but when you step back and see the work and plans of God, you fully understand the meaning of the word *awesome*. To stand on that road and realize that God raised the Roman Empire for the very purpose of getting the good news out to the world gives us a glimpse into the majesty and complexity of His plans. It is no wonder we can't often figure out what He is doing in our lives (except in those instances where He graciously offers us a glimpse), as His ways and His plans are so beyond what we can see that they are truly beyond our comprehension.

So as you walk along the road that is before you (as Peter and Paul did), you can trust that the same One who was guiding their steps will guide yours also, if you will only let Him.

Jesus promised His followers, "In this world you will have trouble." But there is good news, for in the very next breath He says, "But take heart, I have overcome the world" (John 16:33 NIV). That is great news. When you follow Jesus, you have by your side One who has already overcome. He will be with you through your troubles—delivering you from some of them, walking with you through most of them, and eventually bringing you home via one of them.

The joy is that through it all you will never be alone. "And be sure of this: I am with you always, even to the end of the age" (Matt 28:20 NLT).

Stepping-Stones
- Take a moment to realize the complexity, depth, and breadth of God's plan for all of humanity across time and space. Then realize that He has a part for you to play in that plan. Before the foundations of the world were laid in place, you were important to Him.
    - How does that make you feel?
    - How does that affect your ability to trust Him?

Signpost: *A journey of a thousand miles begins with a single step.*

Take Your Next Step

Have you ever challenged a friend to a foot race? Arm wrestle? Duel? (Hopefully not the last one!) When we are challenged with something, we can get a bit of an adrenaline rush and can either be excited or terrified.

Life has all sorts of challenges. Big ones, like getting top marks in school, making the team, landing the dream job, or delivering a baby without drugs. And some not-so-big ones, like making it through a trying day, dealing with rude people, or ordering the salad when you really want the cheeseburger and fries. If there were no challenges in life, it could get pretty boring and you'd find yourself coasting.

Over the past few months, God has been pushing and challenging me, reminding me that He is to be my security and first on my list of priorities. I have learned that when God is directing me, it doesn't matter what is going on around me; I am to be faithful to Him and to follow His leading. The wonderful thing is that He is happy with even a little progress, even a little willingness on my part. I just need to be open to Him and to His direction. Obedience, not excuses, is what we are to offer to Him. And when we do that, no matter how small our efforts seem, He steps in and is there for us, doing much more than we can ask or think. All we need to do is turn back to Him, and He is right there. He never leaves us.

Is God challenging you today? Or has He decided that you just won't listen? I heard someone say once that if people stop telling you things, it isn't because they agree with you. Rather, it is because they have decided that you just won't listen. I don't ever want God to decide that I won't listen. It is time to take that next step, time to grow and go deeper. If you can't identify a current challenge in your life, turn back to Him, seek Him out, and ask Him to take you deeper so you will know more about Him. I'm pretty sure He's not done with you yet and that His desire is for you to grow closer to Him. And get ready because it could be an interesting ride!

Are you facing challenges that seem insurmountable? Or perhaps just a lot of smaller things that are draining and threatening to overwhelm you? Dealing with life's challenges is best done with these two steps: (1) Commit the issue to Jesus, asking for His help; and (2) Then begin to do what you can, focusing on the task immediately before you. Don't allow the enormity of the challenge to get to you. Remember the old saying "A journey of a thousand miles begins with a single step." My dad used to often say it this way: "It is easier to steer a moving vehicle than one that is stopped." So start doing something, and allow God to direct your steps.

The mind of man plans his way. But the LORD directs his steps. (Proverbs 16:9 NASB)

When you are overwhelmed, remember this old joke: "Q: How do you eat an elephant? A: One bite at a time." Tackle your challenges one step at a time, and trust that as you take each step, God will show you the next one to take.

Stepping-Stones

- Are you growing deeper in your relationship with the Lord?

- Are you trusting Him to guide your next step?

- What have you been resisting doing? Pray about it and take a step. Trust that God will be there to direct and guide you.

Signpost: *Good choices produce good results.*

Everything Is Permissible

We spent the evening at the Sandwich Fair in Illinois. It's like the State Fair of Texas, but on a smaller scale, except where the food was concerned. Funnel cakes, corn dogs, pizza, all manner of food-on-a-stick, deep-fried pickles, deep-fried Twinkies, deep-fried … well, you get the picture. Nothing healthy but everything TASTY! But it reminded me of what Paul wrote in 1 Corinthians 10:23: "Everything is permissible" (paraphrase)—but not everything is beneficial. "Everything is permissible"—but not everything is constructive. All that food was permissible, but it certainly was NOT beneficial for my arteries, my waistline, or my cholesterol level!

How many things do we do in life that are permissible but are not beneficial or constructive? I can spend hours surfing the web. Permissible? Sure. Constructive? Not usually. Lately, I've found myself discontented with the things I usually do to unwind or relax. Reading. Watching TV. I'm restless, knowing there has got to be a better way to spend my time. So I caught up on my devotional. Did some prep work for the ladies Bible study. Finished memorizing Psalm 18. Permissible? Of course. Beneficial and constructive? Absolutely. And I felt so much better after doing those things than I ever do reading magazines or watching TV.

Just like eating healthy food is better for your body, filling your mind with the things of God is better for you emotionally and spiritually. So if you find that you are hungry for something substantial, sit down for a meal of scripture once a day and see how your spiritual health improves.

I have heard it said, "If you strive for the things of earth, you will achieve neither them nor the things of heaven. But if you strive for the things of heaven, you'll get both."

Sometimes all we want to do is read a magazine or watch a movie, and there is nothing wrong with that. But I challenge you to put God first. Spend time reading the Bible and praying. You will be amazed how that helps your state of mind and will see real changes in your life. God doesn't tell us to put Him first for His benefit but rather because He knows it will benefit us. In the same manner that a parent instructs a child to look both ways before crossing a street, the instruction is given for the benefit of the one who hears it.

God's instructions are not designed to limit your happiness but rather to increase it by helping you avoid things that will cause you problems.

"Fix your thoughts on what is true, and honorable, and right, and pure, and lovely, and admirable. Think about things that are excellent and worthy of praise" (Philippians 4:8). Whatever we focus on has an impact on our mood and eventually our character. If you are anxious, you have likely taken your focus off God and put it on your environment and surroundings.

Stepping-Stones
- Are you making beneficial choices?

- How do you view Bible reading? If you find it dry, try reading some of the Old Testament stories. If you find it too simplistic, follow the cross-references or find a book on Bible study.

- One-Week Challenge: before you watch TV, read a book or magazine, and even before you exercise, spend five minutes reading the Bible.

- What question/issue do you have in your life that would benefit from some in-depth Bible study?

Signpost: Be careful where you put your trust.

Where Is Your Security?

Woo-hoo! It's PAYDAY today! I've got money again! What a relief! I get to spend it on … oh wait. That's just wrong. I'm putting my security in my paycheck. I am putting my trust in my bank balance, which means I'm living for that special day, twice a month, when I get paid. And what happens when that paycheck is no more? Been there, done that. *Not* fun.

Where is your security?

My emotional security used to be in my husband until we had critical marriage issues and separated for five months. My security had been shattered. God taught me to trust in *Him* during that time. I did, and our marriage was miraculously restored.

My financial security used to be, to some degree, having enough money to live comfortably. Then our company went through drastic change, and we both went without a paycheck for four years (with a bit of cash thrown in here and there when we were absolutely desperate). God taught me that *He* is my Jehovah Jireh ("The Lord Will Provide"). And He did. Every time we needed money and had no idea where it would come from, there was a miraculous provision that we could not explain.

Recently, I've been struggling again with security. Our company had been doing better. There was more money to go around, and I got used to having money available. Then money got tight again, and that old worry came rushing back. It had taken very little time for me to unlearn the lesson that my security is in God.

Then to top it off, after one particularly pitiful/whiny prayer about our lack of money, I opened my devotional, and right there in the middle of the page I read, "God will challenge our security if we don't find it in Him." Whoa.

Do you want your security challenged? I really don't. It's painful, lonely, and makes you squirm. Peace and security come when we trust in God to provide for all our needs. Unlike jobs, money, family, and friends, *He* will never let us down. He provides a foundation that cannot be shaken.

When we begin to worry about finances, we would do well to consider the following sayings of Jesus:

> Consider the lilies, how they grow: they neither toil nor spin, yet I tell you, even Solomon in all his glory was not arrayed like one of these. (Luke 12:27 ESV)

> Your Father in heaven knows what you need before you ask him. (Matthew 6:8 NIV)

So where is *your* security?

Stepping-Stones
- Where is there pressure in your life?
- Are you able to trust God in that area?
- Do an inventory of all that God has done for you in the past. Use that inventory to bolster your trust in Him for your current issue(s).

Signpost: *Forgiveness is a key component of peace.*

Forgiving Others

When I was out of town a few weeks ago, I heard an excellent sermon on forgiveness. The pastor said that he had decided some time ago to forgive everybody all the time. He no longer got offended if someone was rude or inconsiderate. Nor did he hold a grudge. And he felt an incredible sense of freedom.

How often do we become offended at the littlest of things? Some person can cut you off in traffic, and you're ticked the entire drive to work. You tell your coworkers. You think about it off and on throughout the day. All because someone cut you off? What a waste of time and emotions brooding about something like this!

Jesus told a story of the servant who was forgiven a very large debt by his master (10,000 talents, or about 150,000 years worth of wages!). The servant then turned around and refused to forgive a debt owed to him by a fellow servant (100 denarii, or about 100 days worth of wages). His master found out and turned him over to the jailers to be tortured until he could repay the debt. Jesus ends the story with "This is how my heavenly Father will treat each of you unless you forgive your brother from your heart" (Matthew 18:21–35 NIV).

If we forgive everybody all the time, we will have more joy, more peace, and will act more Christlike in our day-to-day lives. More importantly, God will forgive us of our sins. Now, if someone has truly wronged you, it's up to you to decide if you need to speak to that person and resolve the issue or if you can simply forgive and forget. Even if a loved one has broken your trust, you must still forgive them, but you may not be ready to trust them again right away.

> Forgiveness is a command.
> Love is a choice.
> Trust is earned.

I'm going to do my best to forgive everybody all the time. I'm looking forward to the joy and peace that forgiveness will bring.

"Father forgive them" (Luke 23:34 NIV). This scripture sets the bar for the level of forgiveness that we are to strive for in our own lives and dealings with others. The bar has been set quite high. But as with all of God's directives for our lives, this command to forgive is for our own good.

To not forgive will lead to bitterness, loneliness, and anger in your life. Forgiveness, aside from being an act of obedience, is also a step on the path to peace.

Rarely easy, always required, and always to our benefit. If we would approach all of God's instructions with this understanding, our lives would be so much easier.

Is there anyone you have not forgiven?

They might not deserve your forgiveness, but don't you deserve the peace?

Stepping-Stones
- Make a list of people in your life whom you have not forgiven. Here's how to determine if you haven't forgiven them. Think about each person you know (one at a time)

and evaluate the first thought that comes into your mind. If you find unforgiveness, take some time to go through the following steps:

1. Identify what he or she did to you.
2. Acknowledge that to forgive him or her will cost you something. (For example, closure, money, or friendship.)
3. Take time to mourn that loss.
4. Make a conscious choice to forgive him or her.
5. Pray that God will bring your emotions in line with your intellectual decision to forgive.
6. Pray for the person you just forgave.

- You may need to run through these steps repeatedly, but they will eventually lead you to peace and freedom.

Signpost: *Invest time and money in the lives of others.*

Selflessness: The Antidote for a Lonely Life

We are called to live selfless lives, serving others as we do God's will. Easier said than done, right?

As with most things in life, the best way to learn something is to actually do it. Don't just read about it. Don't ask others how they do it. Just do it.

Last week, the members of our church showed their selflessness by pledging a large sum of money, for many a sacrificial amount, to purchase our church building and continue serving the Lord there. What a huge praise!

But let's not stop there. Money is great, no doubt. In fact, it is absolutely necessary. But let's not sit back and congratulate ourselves. Much work is still to be done. And most of it won't cost us a red cent. What it will cost us is time and energy. Time to go out to nearby neighborhoods and tell people about our church. Time to volunteer for the various outreach events our church has every year. Time (and yes, energy!) to teach the kids and the youth. Time and more energy to clean the church building weekly.

We all have extra time in our schedules. I for one could spend a lot less time on my computer and a lot more time doing something that will help to advance God's kingdom. And from a purely selfish standpoint (irony intended), how much better will I feel spending time doing God's work than goofing off?

To be truly selfless, we need to care more about others than ourselves. For some of us (myself included) this will take work! So use Jesus as your example. Find somewhere to volunteer in our church or in your community. Take time for a friend or family member who has been feeling a bit neglected recently. And as you do this, you will become more like Christ, your ultimate goal.

How many opportunities to help others do we pass up on each day?

How many times do we walk by on the "other side" (Luke 10:30–37)?

If you currently volunteer or work in your church, marvelous. Your job is to communicate the joy of such activities to others so they can begin to reach outside themselves.

If the obligations of your life truly keep you too busy, be sure not to let them crush you. Perhaps you can be the reason that someone else reaches outside him- or herself. Don't be afraid to ask for help; that may be the task God has before you right now. It may be your time to be on the receiving end, and then some day you can return the favor.

If you don't know how or where to help, pray about it, and then ask around. It could be that someone is just waiting for you to offer.

Stepping-Stones
- If you are not serving somewhere, why aren't you?
- Are you shy?
    - Find a way to serve on your own (perhaps in the background).
    - Find an outgoing partner and team up with them.

- Are you too busy?
    - Take a close inventory of how you spend your time. Simplify your life to free up some time.
    - Treat your time like you treat your money. Prepare a budget for how you want to spend your time.
    - Perhaps there is something you can give up for just a little while to provide time for some sort of volunteer opportunity.

Signpost: *Don't settle for a superficial life.*

Creating Depth

This week we are currently in Plano, Illinois, working at a client site. At lunch today, we had the opportunity to travel down the main street of Plano and see what Hollywood had created. (It is a set for downtown Smallville in the upcoming Superman movie.) As we reflected on how realistic the shops were—they had built a complete 7-Eleven and a Sears store that had not even been there before—we also thought about the fact that these buildings were simply facades. If you drove down the neighboring streets, you saw naked plywood and two-by-fours with shipping containers piled up behind them for support.

How often do we walk through life like that? A mere shell of what we are supposed to be? Smiling, laughing, and praising God with our words but living a life of "quiet desperation"? Why is it so hard to live our lives with God to the depth that both He and we desire ("For I do not understand my own actions. For I do not do what I want, but I do the very thing I hate" (Romans 7:15 ESV))? Why is it so easy to be superficial, not just with God but also with one another?

In our busy lives, it is very easy to forget about God. Not completely, but as life's little ups and downs crowd around us, it seems that God is easily pushed to the side. We have an enemy who rejoices when that happens. I don't want to ever give our enemy cause to rejoice. I want to take this opportunity to encourage you to dig deeper—dig into the Word, dig into your devotionals, dig into your relationships, and dig into our church. It is the trees with the deep roots that survive the harsh weather and that draw water from the deepest springs.

Drawing close and going deeper. That is what sustains us when life gets in the way.

How often we display a superficial reality to those around us. The clichéd conversational response of "I'm fine" when someone asks how we are, never or rarely risking hurt by giving a truthful or deeper answer. We perceive safety in superficiality, but nothing could be further from the truth. How many people have taken their lives when just hours before they had told someone "I'm fine"? How many marriages have crumbled when one spouse believed that all was well because he or she had never been told otherwise?

Depth brings stability. Depth in the relationships around us provides us with a safe place to go when life's problems assail us. Depth provides a defense against issues because then they can be discussed before they become problems.

Begin to work today to deepen and strengthen your relationships.

Stepping-Stones

- Identify one or two relationships in your life that need to be strengthened.

- Create a plan to strengthen them. Don't start the process with a long talk about the flaws of the relationship. Instead, make plans to spend time with the person, have fun together, and focus on what is already strong in the relationship.

- Then when you have a foundation set on bedrock (and if the flaws haven't fixed themselves by that point), discuss how you can make the relationship even better.

Signpost: Being in God's presence releases joy.

Choose Joy

I just got back to Texas on Tuesday afternoon from a vacation in Canada. I don't know about you, but there is always a letdown when I return from my summer trip to see family. Maybe it's the twenty-one-hour drive. Maybe it's the fact I had to leave family behind (and it's getting harder and harder as our parents age). Maybe it's because I have to do a ton of laundry and then repack for a business trip to Chicago this Saturday. Or maybe it's because it's STILL over one hundred degrees here and it was a good twenty to twenty-five degrees cooler in Canada. (Sigh.)

But as I went about my first day back at work, and all the frustrations that go along with that, Glenn asked if I had made a conscious decision to have joy today. I flippantly replied, "No. I decided to be grumpy!" But he had made a good point. Your day might be lousy for all sorts of reasons, but rather than give in to the anger, frustration, weariness, or sadness, why not decide to have joy instead? But not just any joy—the joy of the Lord. No matter where your life takes you and how much things change, no matter what trials you are undergoing, God is the one thing that is consistent. Jesus said that He came so we might have abundant life and in His presence is fullness of joy. He's always available at a moment's notice. He loves us, no matter what. He will never let us down or disappoint us. It's impossible to always be *happy*, but it's not impossible to always have *joy*.

I chose joy after Glenn's comment. And I felt much better. (Of course, reading through various scriptures for this devotional helped immensely!) Choose joy right now. And then make an effort to choose it every day from now on.

How easy it is for us to forget that we have a choice. It is almost automatic that we let the cares and events of the world choke the joy out of our lives, and with that loss of joy usually goes peace. Our anxieties and fears—some real and some imagined—rise up and obscure our view of the One whose peace and joy we so desperately need.

We cannot control our circumstances, but we can control our responses and choose to focus on Jesus. As Peter so excellently modeled for us, when we focus on Christ, our circumstances don't matter. But when we focus on our circumstances, we begin to drown in them (Matthew 14:25–33).

Our outlook and focus will determine if we walk through life's highs and lows with or without joy.

Stepping-Stones
- Over the next week, I encourage you to make a conscious and deliberate decision (at the start of each day) to choose joy.

- Do some proactive research in the Bible. Find scriptures that relate to joy and have those ready to study when the cares of the world threaten to overwhelm you.

Signpost: Don't put off developing new relationships.

New Relationships

This past week, we visited the Mennonite village near the city where I grew up. (Both sides of my family are Mennonite, and both sets of grandparents came to Canada from Russia.) There were all sorts of demonstrations and displays, and one was a sod house, or semlin, that many Mennonites who came to Canada first lived in since they had to build a home quickly to shelter them from the brutal winters. Oftentimes during the coldest of nights, they would bring their cows into the house with them to provide additional warmth. It was also noted that if they ran out of grain for the cows, the people would share their bread with the cows! The Mennonites were a tightly knit community, and as more emigrated from Russia, those who had come before and had already settled took care of them.

In the sermon in the church we visited on Sunday, the pastor talked about the importance of "breaking bread" with others. "Breaking bread" was a common Jewish expression for the sharing of a meal. They would speak a blessing like this one: "Blessed art Thou, O Lord our God, King of the universe, who bringest forth bread from the earth."

In Acts, when Paul speaks of the new church, he says they broke bread together, prayed together, and praised God and enjoyed fellowship. They helped one another and shared what they could with those in need. And more and more believers were added daily. They knew that the best way to draw people to Jesus was to form relationships with them. When we do life with people, they can see the effect that God has on a person, and if we are living right, that will draw them into a closer relationship with us and a new relationship with Jesus.

When was the last time you "broke bread" with someone other than your family or regular group of friends? (Probably not cows, though.) One thing about our church is we love to eat meals together. (Lunch after church anyone?) Think about inviting someone different to break bread with you this week. It's amazing how we can get to know someone over a meal. By sharing a meal, we can build and strengthen relationships, encourage and pray for one another, and glorify God.

Is there someone with whom you have been meaning to connect? A new neighbor you have meant to visit? Someone in your church you have just never managed to invite for lunch? Take a chance and reach out. Chances are you will be glad that you did.

Many times in my life I have looked back in regret at relationships not formed and lost opportunities to make a friend. Don't make that same mistake. (I know I do my best to not repeat that now.) It might mean stepping out of your comfort zone, but that also is usually a good thing.

Don't neglect your current relationships either. Extend an invitation, offer an apology, or just make an effort.

Pray, asking God who needs you as a friend (or maybe who you need as a friend). Ask Him to bring him or her across your path. And when He does, reach out to him or her. I'm pretty sure you'll be happy with the result.

Stepping-Stones
- What stops you from forming new relationships?

- Fear?
- Laziness?
- Comfort?

- Start simple. Start by deepening one or two relationships. Then when those are solid, branch out together to create new ones.

Signpost: Remember to follow the Golden Rule.

Be Kind to One Another

How is your relationship with God? With your spouse or significant other? How about your friends? How much do you value those relationships? Probably a lot. When things are going well, everybody is happy, life is treating you fairly, and relationships are fun, easy, and rewarding. But have you ever noticed that oftentimes it takes just one small setback, one little disappointment, or one thing not going our way and we turn around and sin against that person or God?

Glenn was on a flight to Chicago Monday and noticed a couple whose seats were apart asking several people if they would mind switching seats so they could sit together. People agreed and shifted, and they achieved their goal. The man put his hand on the woman's knee, and they seemed happy and content. Shortly thereafter, he started to doze, and his foot twitched and kicked her purse, which was under the seat in front of him. She immediately flew into a rage, pushed his leg back, and pinched his arm—hard. He was stunned since he was asleep and didn't know what had happened! She then spent the next fifteen minutes in a total snit, trying to get the dirt off her purse. A beautiful, tender moment between two people ruined. (The remainder of that flight must have been fun. NOT!)

How often do we treat our friends and family like that? Have you heard the phrase "familiarity breeds contempt"? We think nothing of getting after our spouse because he didn't put his socks in the laundry again. We get upset at our friends if they say something innocent and we take it the wrong way. We yell at God, pound on His chest, and complain about the unfairness of it all. Granted, God can take our anger a lot better than our friends and family can, but regardless, the relationship is slightly damaged afterward. Our friends and family are hurt, and though they will likely forgive, it's hard to forget. The funny thing with God is He is not the one who will suffer from our bad behavior. We will. We damage the relationship between God and us. We slink away from Him, upset at our sin, and too proud to seek Him when really we should be running to Him and asking for forgiveness. He always forgives when we ask, and His Word tells us, "As far as the east is from the west, so far has he removed our transgressions from us" (Psalm 103:12 NIV).

Too often we don't value our relationships enough. I've taken my friends for granted at times. I've taken God for granted a lot. I know He's there, I know He loves me, and I know that I am His. But I don't act like it. If I would only grasp how much He has done for me, how much He has sacrificed, how much He loves me, I would be seeking Him night and day, praising Him constantly, and praying without ceasing. I would have far more respect for Him. I've seen people who do this. It's wonderful to see their spirit so full and joyous. I want that! We should all want that. Seek Him, and He will be faithful.

Be kind. Be nice. Pretty simple concept nicely outlined in the Golden Rule (Matthew 7:12). But even simple concepts can be hard to put into practice when it means putting others before ourselves. Yet that is what is required if you want to have a good relationship. Good relationships are built through commitment, contact, and caring. Whether with God or with people, the relationship will only grow if we are willing to make the effort, spend time with the person, and put his or her feelings before our own.

Stepping-Stones
- What relationships have you been neglecting?
    - What can you do to fix that?

- Do you consistently follow the Golden Rule?

- Evaluate the words you say over the next couple of days. Take note of your internal reactions to people and circumstances. Do you habitually react in anger or in love?

Signpost: *Peace is not the absence of trouble. Rather, it is a sense of calm in the midst of trouble.*

Peace in the Storms

We have had some crazy storms in the last week or two with thunder, lightning, rain, hail, wind, and even tornados. Some of us had roof damage, trees down, and even a few hail dents on the hood of the car. But for the most part, the storms lasted a short time and we weathered them pretty well.

What about the storms in your life? Those trials and troubles that we all face? How turbulent are they? How long are they lasting? How are you weathering them? Some might be brief and are over in less than a day. Others can stretch for months or longer. Glenn and I weathered a financial storm for about four years when we started our own company. We literally didn't get paid the first year and then were paid only very little over the next several years. Even though times were extremely tough, we were miraculously able to pay our bills and always had what we needed. Not what we wanted, perhaps, but what we needed. God took care of our needs. He provided as only He can. His Word says, "The righteous person may have many troubles, but the LORD delivers him from them all" (Psalm 34:19 NIV).

How comforting to know that God is not only aware of the troubles and storms we face, but that He will also deliver us from them. Maybe not in our timing. Maybe not in the way we expected. But He is faithful to deliver us.

As you pray about the storms in your life or in the life of a loved one, remember that you are not alone. God is with you in the midst of it. There is an end in sight.

Peace is not the absence of trouble but rather the calm in the midst of trouble. In the same way that you don't need willpower until you face temptation, you have no need for peace until you encounter events that cause anxiety.

In Mark 4:37–40, Jesus was at peace in the storm because His trust was not in the boat or in the men sailing the boat but in God. Because of this, when the disciples woke Him up, He didn't share their anxiety but instead shared God's peace with them.

When you find yourself in a storm, don't look at the storm or your own abilities. Focus on Jesus and rely on Him. He will either calm the storm or He will calm you. He is the only true source of peace. "My peace I give you. I do not give to you as the world gives. Do not let your hearts be troubled and do not be afraid" (John 14:27 NIV).

Stepping-Stones
- What storms have you weathered in your life? What did those storms teach you?

- Remembering what God has done in the past builds our faith and helps us trust Him in our present and future.

- Make a list of how God has protected or delivered you in the past. Keep this list handy and reference it when new storms enter your life.

- Try to identify some lifestyle changes you can make to avoid storms in the future.

- Are there other steps you can take so you will be able to focus more on Jesus and less on the storms?

Signpost: *Learn to trust in God's plan and timing.*

God's Timing

We had a great visit with family back home this past weekend. You may remember a prayer request I sent out a month ago for the safety of my niece's boyfriend, Bill. He was in Tokyo when the earthquake and tsunami hit. I found out when talking to him last weekend that he and the fellows he wrestled with were on a bus coming out of the mountains a half hour out of Sendai. They were high enough up that the tsunami could not reach them. What makes this even more amazing is that they were running thirty minutes late because one of the Japanese wrestlers was running behind. Bill said, "The Japanese are NEVER late, so it was strange." Had they left Tokyo on time, they would have been right in the middle of Sendai where some of the worst earthquake and tsunami damage occurred. And that might have been their time.

Wow. Imagine all the things that had to come into play for the men on that bus to be safe. God's timing never ceases to amaze me. Whenever something like this happens, I always reflect on why God timed it the way He did. Did He want some people who were on that bus to recognize God's awesome power as well as His incredible mercy? Did He want to give them more time if they had not made a decision for Christ yet? For some of us, it's hard to comprehend that God would spare these young men yet allow so many others to perish. Remember that He put the rules in place for the sun to shine, the rain to fall, and, yes, things like tornados, blizzards, earthquakes, and tsunamis to occur. We live in a fallen world, and yes, bad things will happen to good people. But we can have eternal life because of Jesus's sacrifice. Then we don't have to worry when our time comes because we will live for eternity with Jesus in heaven.

I heard someone once say, "God is never late, but He certainly does pass up a lot of opportunities to be early." Our timing and God's timing rarely seem to line up, but we need to realize that His timing is right. Peace comes when we accept that and rest in the knowledge and understanding that He knows more than we do and is in control.

Stress comes when we try to make things happen, when we try to force our timing on a situation. Peace begins when we submit to a loving Father who knows and sees infinitely more than we do.

Sometimes we can look back and understand why things happened in the manner and the timing in which they did. Sometimes we just need to trust. The stronger your relationship with God, the easier it is to trust. Take a look at Psalm 23 for an example of the peace that comes with a strong relationship. We have no need to fear evil when He is with us.

Stepping-Stones
- Make a list of things upon which you are currently waiting. Commit each thing to God.

- Evaluate your part in each item to see if you have done all that you can.
    - If there are things you can still do, get busy and do them.
    - If you have done all that you can, rest in the Lord and in the knowledge that your heavenly Father has this under control.

- Doing these things doesn't mean that things will happen when you want. It doesn't even guarantee that they will happen at all. But it will reassure you and allow you to acknowledge that they are in God's hands now and you need not worry about them any longer.

Signpost: *Sometimes you need to make a specific request for peace.*

Ask for Peace

Wow. We've been so busy lately. Had company in town the last week of March. A user conference the first week of April, followed immediately by a mini vacation to Fredericksburg last weekend. And Thursday we travel back home to Winnipeg for a long weekend visit with family. Bringing Glenn's mom back with us on Monday. Easter weekend following. Then the weekend after, we take his mom to California for a four-day whirlwind tour. Phew! I barely have time to breathe and feel like I am not only *not* catching up but am falling further and further behind! Give me peace, Lord!

It seems like such a simple thing to ask for, but when we're in the thick of things, we don't have time to ask. So we end up like this, staying up late to get work done, rushing around trying to tie up loose ends, and not finding the least bit of relaxation when we're supposed to be on vacation.

Lord, grant us all peace as we move through our busy lives. Help us to take the time to breathe, to take a moment, to *rest* in You. Help us to not put You on our to-do list as something to check off but remind us to take You with us wherever we go and keep You in our hearts and minds constantly. Give Your peace to those who are sick, hurting emotionally, and just need to slow down and rest in You.

Sitting here typing this is my moment of peace, of rest, of spending time with God, and acknowledging that I can't keep up this frenetic pace for much longer. Thank You, Lord, for this moment of calm.

Sometimes our lack of peace is self-inflicted, as we simply overbook and overburden ourselves. Then we wonder why we are stressed out and exhausted all the time. But sometimes it is beyond our control, such as work deadlines, unexpected problems, and sudden illness.

We are promised peace, His peace. We are not promised an absence of problems in this world. In fact, we are promised the opposite (John 16:33). Peace is calm in the midst of the storm, not the absence of a storm.

Are you in a storm right now? Are you stressed or anxious about something in your life? Most people seem to move through life from one stressful/anxious situation to another.

We need to do our part and be wise with our time commitments. But we also need to look to Jesus for the peace that He promises. We need to consider the lilies, realize that we truly have no control, and give our problems to God. Let Him handle the impossible while we work on the possible (even if that is just asking Him for help).

Stepping-Stones
- If you seem to move from one stressful event to another and are always short on time, you might benefit from incorporating some time management techniques into your life.

- God will give us peace if we rest in Him. But if our lives are so jam-packed that we can't even find the time for that, we likely need to simplify or reorganize our lives.

- If this describes your life, I encourage you, with the help of some time-management and/or priority-setting techniques, to remove the unnecessary things from your life. Then spend some of that freed-up time with God.

Signpost: *Changing your focus through prayer.*

Look Outside Yourself

I've been thinking a lot about family this past week, as Glenn's brother and sister-in-law drove down from Canada for a visit. What a sacrifice for them (a twenty-two-hour drive!) and a blessing to us to have them with us last week. Mind you, there was still snow on the ground and below-freezing temps where they live, so maybe it was not such a sacrifice ...

But living so far away from our families and only seeing them a few times a year makes me appreciate my church family so much. We share many holidays and vacations with some of them, and they are there for us during good times and bad.

Many of you are blessed to live close to your extended families, and some of you, like us, have family spread across the country or even in another country! So this week, pray for your family, biological, spiritual, and church. Love them as Christ loves us, and bear with them as Christ bears with us.

Left to our own devices, we are generally selfish creatures. Our views and thoughts turn inward, and we move, more and more, toward evaluating everything with regard to our own comfort. For instance, when we get cut off, we react by thinking, *Why did he cut me off?* We don't look at the situation and think, *I wonder what is wrong in his life that makes him in such a hurry?*

When we look outward, when we give preference to one another (Romans 12:10), we begin to see that our issues may not be as bad as we think. It is akin to picking at a scab—the more you pick (look inward) the less healing takes place. But when you change your focus (from inward to outward), you will find that healing begins to take place in your life, as you miraculously will realize that everyone else's actions are not designed to cause you pain. With that realization comes the ability not to be offended, and if you are not offended, you won't dwell on the issue. Things that used to cause you anxiety will become like "water off a duck's back."

One of the best ways to change your focus is to pray for others. Pray for family, for friends, for all those who cross your path in ways both good and bad. We are specifically told to "Pray for those who persecute you" (Matthew 5:44 NIV). We are told to do that because God knows that as we do so, the anger, frustration, and anxiety that we feel about that person and situation will melt away. By praying for those around you, you release God's blessing in their lives and God's peace in your own.

Stepping-Stones
- Make a point of not taking people for granted.

- Send someone a note or give him or her a call to let him or her know he or she is appreciated.

- Ask someone how you can pray for him or her.

- In any heated encounter, pray before you speak.

Signpost: You are free in Christ.

Celebrate Your Freedom

On July 4, Americans celebrated their freedom (and those who are not American citizens celebrated the fact that we are free to live and work in this country). We are so used to the freedom that we take it for granted. I don't think we fully understand what it means to live in a society where we are free to work where we want, live where we want, and worship how we want.

We have a missionary friend whose heart is for those in Asia who are persecuted for being Christians. He goes on two or three trips a year to bring Bibles and money but mostly to support and encourage the people who are at the forefront of the Christian movement. Many of his friends have been killed for spreading the gospel, and others have gone into hiding to protect their families. These people do not have the benefit of living in the freedom we so richly enjoy here.

However, they have another kind of freedom: freedom in Christ. They are willing to risk their lives to live for Christ. Once they have found Him, they are never letting Him go. They go to great lengths to not only protect themselves and other believers from persecution, but they also, very carefully and prayerfully, seek out others who they believe are also seeking that same freedom and share the good news of Christ with them. The stories our missionary friend brings back from the frontlines, as it were, are both terrifying and inspiring. We are afraid to tell our neighbors about Christ for fear of rejection or ridicule, yet they are willing to tell their neighbors at the risk of being imprisoned, tortured, or killed. Paul says, "For to me, to live is Christ and to die is gain" (Philippians 1:21 NIV). Lord, help me to have that kind of faith.

While we celebrate the freedom we have living in both Canada and the United States, don't forget to (daily) celebrate and praise God for the freedom He has given us. Galatians 5:1 says, "It is for freedom that Christ has set us free. Stand firm, then, and do not let yourselves be burdened again by a yoke of slavery" (NIV). We do not need to be enslaved by our past failures, current trials, or fears. The enemy wants us to dwell on our past failures. (And they are legion, aren't they?) He would like nothing better than for us to focus on our mistakes and make us believe the lie that God could never love us or never really forgive us for the things we have done. Each one who buys into the lie that we are not truly free of our past and our sins is taken out of the evangelism pool by our guilt, adding one more roadblock to winning people for the kingdom.

When you confess, you are forgiven. When you repent, it is remembered no more. When you are tempted to dwell on (or for some of us wallow in) your sins and failures, remember who wants you to do that. It isn't our Father; it is our enemy. So as we celebrated our political freedom today, we must remember every day to hold fast to our spiritual freedom.

It is so easy to allow our thoughts to drag us down into depression and inactivity. Fear, shame, regret—they all stifle our efforts and make us feel unworthy of the task of telling people about Jesus. But we need to evaluate our thoughts (2 Corinthians 10:5). If we find they are false, we must throw them away.

Stepping-Stones
- What thoughts drag you down? Write them down and then dig into the Bible for truth to refute them. Here is a start:
    - "I am unlovable." "For God so loved the world [loved YOU] ..." (John 3:16).
    - "I am too far gone. There is no way back." "Neither height, nor depth ..." (Romans 8:39). Nothing in you or in the world around you can keep God from loving and accepting you if you turn to Him. "But to all who believed him and accepted him, he gave the right to become children of God" (John 1:12 NLT).

Signpost: Working at becoming more like Jesus—pressing on toward perfection.

You Only Fail When You Stop Trying

The other day, I was talking to my mom, who is in her eighties and has been a Christian for over forty years. She was telling me that recent circumstances in her life have given God the opportunity to show her just how much the sinful nature is still inside her. And if you knew my mom, the idea that she still has a lot of the sinful nature left inside her would really put you into a state of depression with regard to your own nature.

But of course she is right. No matter how long we live on this earth, or how long we serve the Lord, we will continue to battle our sinful nature. Just look at Paul's comments in Romans 7:15: "I don't understand myself at all, for I really want to do what is right, but I don't do it. Instead, I do the very thing I hate" (NLT). So if Paul struggled with this, and my mom is still struggling with this, I'm thinking that I am doomed to struggle with this for as long as I live. But I guess the secret really is to not stop struggling; rather, we should always strive to be better, to be more like Jesus. It is when we give up that we have a problem.

So anyway, this past weekend, Sandy took me to a tiger preserve (they rescue tigers that no one wants anymore or that have been abused), and we got a behind-the-scenes tour. They are, in my opinion, one of God's most beautiful creatures, but that isn't the point. One of the tigers there was abused when she was young. Apparently, the subhuman (more on this later) who owned her used her to teach his pit bulls how to fight so they would do better in the dogfights. That's not all he did, but you get the idea. Needless to say, my reaction (see the "subhuman" comment earlier) was not one that God would have me display. Now, while I do believe that there is a case to be made for righteous anger in this situation, I know that my reaction goes beyond that. In reality, I would want this individual to die for what he did to this tiger, not to mention what he was doing to his dogs. And that is not right. (Sigh.)

Jesus died for him just as He died for me. Before I was graciously saved, I was heading for the same hell that this person is most likely heading. Jesus loves him as much as He loves me. So wretched as I am (see sinful nature discussion in the first two paragraphs), how dare I stand and condemn someone else, right? But even knowing all that, I have a hard time changing my opinion and desire for the fate of this person.

So I have a long way to go. I need to learn to hate the sin and the one who drew this man into that sin. Our fight is not with the people of this world (Ephesians 6:12). I am not called to hate this man. I am called to love him. And at the moment, that is a requirement I find very, very difficult to live up to. One day I will. I even made a point of praying for him today because that is what Jesus would want me to do.

I have a long way to go (and I'm guessing that you do to). But as long as we keep trying, as long as we keep drawing closer to Jesus, we will make progress. And I believe that even our stumbling steps toward righteousness bring a smile to His face. There was a line from the song "Mansion Builder" that was popular in my youth by a group called the 2nd Chapter of Acts, which was "Why should I worry; Why should I fret, 'Cause I've got a mansion builder who ain't through with me yet."

The Lord is still working on each and every one of us. He is not yet finished building you or me into a mansion worthy to be called His home. But I am infinitely grateful that He views the shack that I am as worthy enough to move in anyway and do the renovations from the inside.

Stepping-Stones
- Identify one area where you need to improve. (Perhaps you are impatient; perhaps you worry.)
    - Once you have identified that area, identify one application of that flaw (e.g., impatient with your spouse or worried about finances).
    - Then pray about that, and with God's help, work to improve in that area.

- Identify any roadblocks that stand between you and God and work to remove them.

- Have you given up struggling against issues in your life that draw you away from God? Reach out and ask for His strength. We can't do it alone, but it can be done if we let Him work with and through us. As it says in Matthew 19:26, "With man this is impossible, but with God all things are possible" (NIV).

Signpost: We need to learn to hear the still, quiet voice of God.

Where Are You Going?

This question can be asked in a variety of contexts, from a simple request regarding a destination to the idea of career and relationships to the more profound context of eternity. In any context other than the most mundane, our answer should be "Where God leads." But then the question comes "How do you know where that is?"

This is a question I have been asking about my life and career since my friend went to work for Voice of the Martyrs. Before working at VOM, he maintained web pages for hotels. But now he is doing a job that will help spread the good news to the ends of the earth. Made me think. Now, even though I know missionaries couldn't go to the ends of the earth if there were not people back home providing them with support, it still made you think, *Where am I going with my career, with my life?*

The sermon at our church on Sunday made the point that if you don't know what to do, talk to the Holy Spirit, who after all is called the Counselor. Good advice. When was the last time you asked what you should be doing? When was the last time you heard that still, quiet voice gently guiding you?

> If any of you lacks wisdom, you should ask God, who gives generously to all without finding fault, and it will be given to you. (James 1:5 NIV)

And would you recognize God's voice if you heard it? To truly answer that, we need to determine what it takes to recognize a voice. Well, when you get a phone call from someone you know well, you don't have to ask who it is. The better you know someone, the easier it is to recognize his or her voice.

> My sheep hear My voice, and I know them, and they follow Me. (John 10:27 NKJV)

So if you want to be able to hear and recognize His voice, you need to get to know His voice. So when I ask (or when you ask), "Where am I going, Lord?" you'll be able to discern His voice in the noise that is your day-to-day life.

Stepping-Stones
- Have you heard God's voice in your life? That subtle or not-so-subtle guiding influence when facing a decision? The steps you take to learn to hear His voice are the same as those you have been practicing as you have worked through this book. But in this case, the goal is to hear His response. Here are four steps that will help you learn to recognize His voice. This will take time and repetition, but I encourage you to not give up.
    1. Get to know Him. Spend time reading and studying your Bible.
    2. Talk to Him. Spend time in prayer.
    3. Ask to hear from Him specifically. Ask Him to speak to you.
    4. Spend time quietly waiting for a response.

Signpost: *You are the only Bible some people may read.*

What Do People See?

Ever feel like you're being watched? Well, guess what? You are. By your spouse, your kids, your friends, even perfect strangers. People are always watching to see how you act in your day-to-day life. After all, it's pretty easy to act Christlike when things are going great, but do your reactions change when life throws you a curve ball?

Friends of ours recently lost their retirement home to a fire. It burned to the ground; there was nothing to salvage. Thankfully, no one was hurt. It turns out that tradespeople were in the house that day adding more insulation, and the fire investigators determined that the fire had started in the attic. Our friends were devastated, but rather than placing blame, they *prayed* with the people responsible for the fire. That's right, they prayed with them. The fellow who was in the house adding insulation was so upset that he could not sleep or eat since the fire. As they prayed with him, they urged him to go back to church, and he did. I marvel at their strong faith that they can pray with the person who destroyed their dream home. I don't know if I could display this type of witness, but I sure hope I could.

There was another happy side effect from this. My friend's father is not saved, and although he has been told about the Lord, he has not accepted Him. But he too has noticed their great faith. If a fire and my friends' reaction to it is what it takes to bring him to Christ, it will all be worth it.

Life is going to be hard. It's not a matter of *if* you go through trials; it's *when*. John 16:33 says, "I have said these things to you, that in me you may have peace. In the world you will have tribulation. But take heart; I have overcome the world" (ESV). God has overcome the world. We can rely on Him to get us through the tough times.

Are you prepared to put your best foot forward and weather those trials with a strong and steady faith that gets noticed? Will you put your trust in God and let His grace flow into and out of you?

"You are the only Bible some people may read." That is an old saying, but there is a lot of truth in it. To draw people to Jesus, we need to show the world that there is something different about us. And there should be something different. After all, we have direct access to the One who created everything. "Behold, I am the Lord of all flesh, is anything too hard for me?" (Jeremiah 32:27 NASB). That should cause us to live our lives differently.

There can and should be a peace and a joy that reflects from us that will lead an anxious and depressed world to the One who has loved it since before time began.

Stepping-Stones
- Starting this week, make an effort to reflect the peace and joy of the Lord, realizing that to do so you need to spend time in His presence.

- When things happen this week, take a moment before you react. Then make an effort to *respond* in a manner that reflects the character of Christ.

- One practical way you can remind yourself to do this (and it really works in my life) is to wear a cross on a necklace or a ring or somewhere else. You'll be amazed how your behavior changes when you are advertising that you follow Christ.

Signpost: *Our actions affect our relationships.*

Get Clean

I was reading a devotional on Leviticus 15 that talks about all the things that can make a person ceremonially unclean. It describes the process of cleansing oneself and offering sacrifices before being able to approach a holy God.

You might read that and think, *Thank goodness for Jesus, who fulfilled the law and now we live under grace. We don't have to worry about ceremonial cleansing before we go to God.* Although it's true we don't have to wash ourselves and wait until the evening before we are once again clean, this can still be applied to our lives today.

Ceremonial cleansing from the Old Testament can be likened to removing sin from our hearts today. What is in your life today that is making you unclean? Before our relationship can be fully right with God, we must confess our sins and get our hearts right. Pride, idolatry, gossip, lying, (insert sin here) contaminates our hearts and separates us from God.

In Leviticus 15:31, God says, "You must keep the Israelites separate from things that make them unclean, so they will not die in their uncleanness for defiling my dwelling place, which is among them" (NIV).

What do you need to remove from your life? What sin has taken up residence in your heart? "Search me, God, and know my heart; test me and know my anxious thoughts. See if there is any offensive way in me, and lead me in the way everlasting" (Psalm

139:23–24 NIV). You need to serve an eviction notice and make sure that you are doing all you can to keep your conscience clear.

Once you have removed the sin from your life, you will be clean and can have unhindered fellowship with God. First Peter 1:14–16 says, "As obedient children, do not conform to the evil desires you had when you lived in ignorance. But just as he who called you is holy, so be holy in all you do; for it is written: 'Be holy, because I am holy'" (NIV).

We know there is nothing we can do on our own that will remove our sin. We are unable to become clean using our own resources. But we can at least dust ourselves off. Our relationship with Jesus is just that, a relationship, and while His sacrifice makes the relationship possible, our actions can affect the quality of that relationship.

Think about human relationships, for instance. If you have done something of which your spouse would not approve, that will hang between you even if he or she doesn't know about it. In the same way, if you are feeling guilty in God's presence, the peace that His presence should bring will elude you.

One step on the road to peace is to get clean. Just say, "I'm sorry."

Stepping-Stones
- Is there anything in your life that you are hiding from God?
- Is there anything for which you need to apologize to the people in your life?
- Evaluate your actions and the health of your relationships, and work to improve both.

Signpost: *Take some time to really study what you read.*

Paraphrase

This week in our Bible study we learned a new technique for studying the Bible. It's called "Paraphrase It." That is pretty self-explanatory. You take a passage of the Bible, read it until you understand what it is saying, and then reword it, using your own words. What I am finding is that when I combine Bible study with prayer (even if I sometimes forget to pray), God comes up with some really neat stuff.

The first two days of the week have been really interesting. Each time I have paraphrased the given verses, the result has been rather odd and yet quite meaningful. Whenever I get results like that I am always excited because it is then that I realize I didn't have a whole lot to do with the result.

The first verses we were to paraphrase were from James 1:2–4: "Consider it pure joy my brothers, whenever you face trials of many kinds, because you know that the testing of your faith develops perseverance. Perseverance must finish its work so that you may be mature and complete, not lacking anything" (NIV).

My paraphrase was "When things are not going the way that you want, STOP! And realize that you are being groomed for greatness."

We are being groomed for heaven and to spend eternity with Jesus. Remember when your mom used to comb the knots out of your hair? It hurt, but the end result looked pretty good. So when trials and troubles come into your life, it may help to think that you are getting some tangles worked out and to remember that you are being groomed for greatness.

The next day, the verses were James 1:19–20: "My dear brothers, take note of this: Everyone should be quick to listen, slow to speak and slow to become angry, for man's anger does not bring about the righteous life that God desires" (NIV).

My paraphrase was "Before you get mad, ask yourself, 'Did I really hear what I thought I heard? Did I fully listen to the whole story? Is what I heard dangerous (does it need to be stopped)?' If you can be angry at the situation and not at the person, address the situation and right the wrong by any means available. Otherwise, swallow your pride and keep your mouth shut."

Now, whether you like or agree with my paraphrase really isn't the point. Rather, the point is that as I studied and reviewed the scripture, I gained some interesting and informative insights. These insights may have just been for me (or maybe they speak to you too), but the really cool thing is that in order for me to write what I did, God had to be involved, and that is exciting. And that wouldn't have happened if I hadn't been spending time studying the Bible.

I have heard it said that the difference between reading the Bible and studying the Bible is whether or not you are writing anything down. I find that when I take the time to write out something, it forces me to think on it more than it does when I simply read it. Both activities are important, but I have learned a lot when I realized that they are distinct activities.

Stepping-Stones
- Spend some time studying the Bible. Paraphrasing scripture is a great place to start. Try these verses. Perhaps what you write down will surprise you.
    - John 3:16
    - John 1:1–5
    - Romans 8:6

Signpost: The habit of Bible study and prayer

A Wise Use of Time

Wow, life gets busy. This week I was out of town on business, so I was working long hours, dining with the client (okay, so not all the parts of my job are hard), and getting back to the hotel in time to crash and then begin it all again. I did get some of my study in, and I enjoyed it. It really is fun (and like I said before, worth it). But it always seemed to be something I was struggling to work into my schedule.

Then life got boring. I came home last night in the rain and the lightning. We landed early, so all should have been wonderful, right? Wrong. For safety reasons (that I fully support), the ground crew cannot work if there is lightning. So we sat, waited, moaned, and groaned for two and a half hours on the tarmac. I tried to pray. I did pray if you count "God, PLEEEASE get us a gate and stop the lightning!" But my mind was certainly not in the place to study the Bible. Looking back on it now, I missed a great opportunity to do some Bible reading. But in the heat of the moment, I wasn't thinking that way.

So why am I sharing this with you? Well, I guess it is to highlight that whether you are too busy or have too much free time on your hands, you still need to work into your life the habit and discipline of Bible study and prayer so when you have no time, you make the time, and when you have too much time (even if it is on a hot, crowded airplane), your first instinct is to meet with God. I wasted two hours last night; hopefully, I'll be smarter next time. My dad always said that we should learn from other people's mistakes because we don't have time to make them all ourselves. So learn from mine, and always be ready to take advantage of the time you have to spend time reading and studying the Bible. That is never a waste.

Have you ever wondered why pastors and religious books always harp on spending time reading the Bible? I believe it is because they have learned what it does in their lives. Someone once told me that BIBLE stands for "Basic Instructions Before Leaving Earth." It's a funny little thought, but one that has some wisdom hidden within it. It is certainly our best method of learning the character of God and getting a proper picture of who He is. Without it, we are left with only sound bites and other people's opinions, both of which can quickly lead to misunderstandings. As we learn more about God, we get our perspective on life reset, our priorities realigned, and our foundation firmed up. All because we begin to see God as He truly is. I heard a pastor say that if we are underwhelmed by Jesus (which comes from an incomplete knowledge of His character and who He is), we will be overwhelmed by our circumstances. But if we (by getting a clearer view of who Jesus is) become overwhelmed by Jesus, we will be underwhelmed by our circumstances. That understanding and perspective is a huge step on the pathway to peace.

Stepping-Stones
- Look for opportunities throughout the coming week for time when you can pray or study.

- There are many times in a normal day when you can work in some prayer and move toward a life where you are praying "without ceasing."

- The next time you are waiting in line, pray for the clerk and the people in line with you.
- The next time you are waiting to meet with someone, read the Bible.

Signpost: *We need to understand that God is limitless.*

Limitless Life

A few weeks ago, I read an article entitled "15 Things You Should Give Up To Be Happy." It was really interesting, and one of the items in the list really resonated with me.

The item was "Give up your limiting beliefs." How often do we put God in a box? How many times have we thought, *That's just too hard. I can't do it?* We forget that God can do anything, and yes, in our own strength there are many things we can't do, but with God's strength and will, we can do anything He has set in place for us. God caused the sun to stand still so Joshua could finish the battle and defeat his enemies. Jesus brought people back from the dead. Do you still think that God is limited? Philippians 4:13 reminds us, "I can do all this through him who gives me strength" (NIV).

For us to truly understand what is meant when we are told not to limit God, we need to catch a glimpse of His majesty, complexity, and infinity. One way to do this is to look at the word *predestined*. This word causes many issues, as people struggle to reconcile the gift of free will with the concept of predestination. The irony of that struggle is that it only becomes a struggle because of our rules of syntax and the limits we put on God. Let me explain. When we look at the word *PREdestined,* some take this to mean that free will is a myth and that God is capricious and has handpicked His followers (thus deliberately condemning the rest to hell). The issue is that people have created theological statements and beliefs not based on the character and person of God but on grade-school rules of grammar. The issue is that in many (if not all) languages, verbs have a tense, and that tense is predicated on the concept of time. For example:

- I ran. (past)
- I will run. (future)
- I am running. (present)

It is not possible to write a grammatically correct sentence, in English anyway, without an explicit or implicit time component.

But God is not bound by time. C. S. Lewis in his book *The Screwtape Letters* states that time exists simply because we are unable to comprehend God's unbounded NOW. God's view is not limited by time. He is, by His very nature, limitless.

So when the word *PREdestined* is used, we would do better to replace it with "that which God knew before you did because from His point of view, expressed in human language, it has already happened." So God doesn't pick and choose who gets saved, but rather sees the decisions that, from that person's point of view, have not yet been made.

When we begin to understand the limitlessness that is God, we will be able to trust Him and to live our lives without the limits imposed by fear, ignorance, or anxiety because we will know that when it comes to our future, our Father is already there.

Stepping-Stones
- Take a moment and mull over the idea that God is outside of time. If you try to dissect it too much, you'll find that it isn't something you can truly understand. But it will hopefully be something you can come to accept.

- Look up the words like *predestined* and *predetermined* in the Bible. Read them with the new understanding that they do not take away free will.

- God is not surprised. Nothing happens in your life that He didn't already know was going to happen, that He hasn't already worked into the plan He has for your life.

- Use this idea (God outside of time) to alleviate any worries you may have about your future. Take some time and give those worries to God. Then rest in the knowledge that He isn't surprised by the eventual outcome. While you don't know what the future will bring, you can know you are loved by the One who does. And regardless of what the future does bring, you need to cling to the character of God and trust Him.

Signpost: *Not forgiving someone is like taking poison in the hope that someone else will die.*

Forgiveness

We have a sign in our house that says, "Forgive everyone everything all the time." Wise words and yet another step on the path to peace. Forgiveness is something we are commanded to do, but so often we find it hard to do. So many scriptures come to mind telling us to forgive one another.

> Bear with each other and forgive one another if any of you has a grievance against someone. Forgive as the Lord forgave you. (Colossians 3:13 NIV)

> Then Peter came to Jesus and asked, "Lord, how many times shall I forgive my brother or sister who sins against me? Up to seven times?" Jesus answered, "I tell you, not seven times, but seventy-seven times." (Matthew 18:21–22 NIV)

> And when you stand praying, if you hold anything against anyone, forgive them, so that your Father in heaven may forgive you your sins. (Mark 11:25 NIV)

I am not the quickest to forgive when I feel I've been wronged. For some reason, I like to fume for a while and wallow in my anger. But we give Satan a foothold the longer we have unforgiveness in our hearts, and that's why it sometimes seems so hard to forgive someone. But God's Word says it best in Matthew 6:14–15, "For if you forgive other people when they sin against you, your heavenly Father will also forgive you. But if you do not forgive others their sins, your Father will not forgive your sins" (NIV). (If that second sentence doesn't get your attention, I don't know what will.)

Unforgiveness is a great lie of our enemy, and one that many people buy into. It begins with our believing that we have the right to something, and when that right is infringed upon, we have the right to be angry and to stay angry until our rights are restored and some penalty (to the offending party) has been inflicted.

I once heard unforgiveness defined as "punishing yourself for someone else's crimes." That is so true because when we hold onto an offense and refuse to forgive, all we manage to do is build up resentment and bitterness in our own lives, which just leads to even more damage to ourselves while leaving the offending party unscathed.

When you fail to forgive, or rather when you choose not to forgive, you only hurt yourself. God knows that, and it is for that reason He tells us to forgive.

So how about it? Have anybody you need to forgive today? Do they deserve your forgiveness? Do we deserve God's forgiveness?

Do it now.

Stepping-Stones
- Often it is hard to forgive, but it can still be a choice. If you are having trouble forgiving, try these steps. (We have addressed these before, but this is such an important concept, it is worth repeating.)
    - Identify what they did to you.
    - Acknowledge that to forgive them will cost you something. (For example, closure, money, or friendship.)

- Take time to mourn that loss.
- Make a conscious choice to forgive them.
- Pray that God will bring your emotions in line with your intellectual decision to forgive.
- Pray for the person you just forgave.

• Our goal should be that these steps become so ingrained in us that we run through them immediately, or very soon after, we have been hurt or offended.

Signpost: There are many around you whose lives are broken, and they need your prayers.

Hell on Earth

Over the past few weeks, it seems as if multiple tragedies have hit people around us. From fires to thefts, sickness to surgeries, people are being battered by life on every side. I am so grateful that we have a Lord who looks out for us, a Lord who "prays for us, that we will not falter" (Luke 22:32). Admittedly, we would rather have one that simply made our life easy and perfect, but that's not how it works. Sometimes we ask why even though the question itself is nothing but a waste of time. "The Lord directs our steps, So why try to understand everything along the way?" (Proverbs 20:24 NLT). But always we have Someone with us who can carry us when things go bad.

On my way into work last week in Chicago was a woman standing at the bus stop at a corner where we were stopped at a red light. She was screaming into her cell phone, cursing up a blue streak at someone on the other end. What I couldn't see at first (but Sandy did) was that this woman's little girl was sitting on the bench behind her, looking up at her mom with wide, scared eyes. Seeing the little girl broke our hearts, and we took some time to pray for her. (Please do the same as you read this.) But upon reflection, I realized that our hearts should also break for the woman on the phone. Obviously her life is broken: broken relationships, broken promises, broken dreams, and broken hopes. She is trying to go through life on human power alone. She doesn't have someone to carry her, or rather, she hasn't been told that she actually does have Someone who is willing to carry her. How terribly sad.

So often when we pray for the salvation of those around us, we are centered on simply wanting them to have the right address for eternity; a heaven versus hell thing. That is good; we should have that focus. But what I realized last week is that many people are suffering through their own personal hell, right here and right now. They don't know that they have a Savior who is waiting for them to answer His call (Revelation 3:20). They don't know that there is actually a source of hope, joy, and peace that goes beyond anything they can even begin to imagine.

This is meant to be an encouragement, an impetus to perhaps add understanding to your prayers for the lost. It isn't simply that we should pray that they don't spend eternity in hell, but rather, we should pray that they don't spend another second in the hell in which they are currently living. To be without a Savior, without someone who is Lord of your life, is scary. That is the very meaning of hopeless and the very definition of hell.

Who in your life needs the Lord? Create a list, and commit to pray for them. There is nothing you can do that is more important.

Make a special effort to show them the love of Jesus. The unsaved don't need our judgment; they need our love and help. If someone were drowning, we wouldn't spend time lecturing him or her on the importance of knowing how to swim before throwing a life preserver. So why would we do that when people are drowning in their sin? Jesus came to seek and save the lost, not to berate and judge them. If He took that approach, don't you think that we should too?

Pray. Pray for the lost. Their lives and their souls are depending on you.

Stepping-Stones

- Make a list of three people you know who need Jesus. Commit to pray for them each day for a month (or longer), and trust God for the result.

- As the credits roll for your favorite TV show, pray for the actors so they would become Christians.

- When you see people throughout your day who are angry or suffering, take just a moment and pray for them.

Signpost: *Take the time to put God first in your life.*

Stuff

A couple of weeks ago, Sandy and I heard a sermon entitled "Overwhelmed." Given what has been happening at work, we figured it would be exactly what we needed to hear. It was a good sermon, nothing we hadn't heard before—the whole concept that God should be first in your life. Let me pause here; I am actually quite terrible in my consistency of Bible reading and quiet time. In fact, truth be told, I am quite consistent in missing it. As I am not a morning person, I don't want to get up any earlier than I have to, so I plan and intend to read my Bible in the evening or when I get home from work. How often do you think things come up that derail that plan?

So the pastor was talking about putting God first and I'm thinking, *Yeah, I need to do that.* But then he said something that hit me: if you put God first, God will take care of all the "stuff" in your life. (And if you don't put Him first, that "stuff" crowds Him out of your life.) I realized that was something I desperately needed given how overwhelmed I had been feeling. Of course, this wasn't a new concept, but my skull is so thick that God has to beat things through it before it gets to my brain.

The pastor challenged us to put God first and let Him handle the "stuff" in the coming week. So we did. It wasn't easy, but it wasn't terribly hard either. It was amazing how often the chapter I read related to what I needed to hear. In fact, one morning I let my e-mails push God out of the way. I received an annoying e-mail from a client, and I replied rather tersely. (I was professional; I just wasn't nice.) Then I realized I hadn't read the Bible, so I went to the Internet and pulled up a Bible site. "By chance" I decided to read James 3 (mostly because I didn't want to read James 1). Well, after reading that, I had to send another e-mail to that client, and this one was much nicer. When you read James 3, substitute "tongue" with "fingers and keyboard" and you'll see why I had to send a second e-mail.

As the week progressed, both Sandy and I actually did really well in putting God first. On Friday, we went out for lunch and I asked her how her day had gone. (We work six feet apart, and I had no idea how her morning had gone. That gives you a look at how busy we had been.) She said something along the lines of "Well, I was busy today, but I think I have everything done now that I needed to do." I responded that I still had stuff to do, but that everything seemed to be nicely under control. She looked thoughtful and said, "Wow, and we were so overwhelmed at the start of the week." Even now I get chills as I relate this. My jaw dropped open, and I asked her, "What did you say?" As we continued to talk, we realized that we were no longer overwhelmed. Busy, yeah. Overworked, probably. But no longer drowning.

And I was surprised. I was stunned, grateful, and happy, but still surprised. Why am I surprised when God does what He says He'll do? I guess part of it is because so often "His ways are not [my] ways" (Isaiah 55:9) and I get used to Him not doing what I want that I begin to think He won't help me. Wow, that sounds even worse when I type it out and re-read it. But I guess it's true.

So I would encourage you to put God first. It really is worth it. (And I do mean first. Do some Bible reading in the morning.) Also, don't be surprised when He shows up. Rather, wait expectantly because He will show up. "But as for me, I will watch expectantly for the Lord; I will wait for the God of my salvation. My God will hear me" (Micah 7:7 ASV).

We are promised that when we wait upon the Lord, our strength will be renewed (Isaiah 40:31 KJV). But how easy it is to get so busy and to not have time to do just that. The irony is that we are likely feeling busy because we don't actually spend that time with God.

Stepping-Stones
- Find a reading plan for the Bible. (Start small. Try one week.)
- Spend that first week reading the assigned scriptures.
- Then the next week, read them again. But this time, take some notes, look up some cross-referenced scriptures, and pray.
- In this way, you'll see the difference between merely reading the Bible and studying the Bible. If you want to advance beyond that, add some prayer time before and after you study.

Signpost: *Involve God in all aspects of our lives.*

Sometimes Smart Isn't Smart Enough

I find this expression funny: "Better to be lucky than smart." But this week, I got a fantastic lesson in the fact that it is far better to be prayerful than smart. I had been out of town helping a client upgrade our software. That trip was absolutely covered in prayer, and although there were a few minor hiccups, it went wonderfully well.

While I was on the plane home, they started having real troubles with one aspect of the system. I was unavailable, but they got in touch with the guy I work with who built the system. He is one of the two most brilliant technical people I know, but sadly he is not a Christian. When I got home, I found out that he was working on the issue, so I figured all would be well in the morning. I did pray a rather strange prayer, saying, "Lord, please help him fix this. Although he won't give you the glory, I will."

The next morning, I found that he had worked on it most of the night and had narrowed it down so we could replicate the problem, but the problem still existed. My stress level at this point was getting very high because this meant that my client couldn't run his business properly. So again I began to pray. At times like this, I pray deeply theological prayers like "Please help me!" Using the information my colleague had uncovered overnight, I began to work and pray, and within about half an hour, I was able to uncover the piece of information that allowed him to fix it.

How did I uncover it? I played a hunch. A hunch that no one will ever be able to convince me wasn't divinely inspired. And that hunch led to information, and that information allowed my colleague to fix the problem. It turns out that quite likely this was the same problem (which had been impossible to diagnose) that another client was experiencing.

Well, lesson learned. Better to be prayerful than smart. So as you go through your tasks day by day and week by week, remember to involve God. The Bible states, "You do not have because you do not ask" (James 4:2b NASB) and "If any of you lacks wisdom, you should ask God, who gives generously to all without finding fault, and it will be given to you" (James 1:5 NIV). I am quickly coming to the conclusion that I can do nothing without God.

So don't wait until you are desperate. Involve God from the start and save yourself a whole lot of frustration and suffering in the process. And then remember to thank Him and give Him all the glory. I told Him that I would, and by writing this, I think I have kept up my end of the bargain.

So many times, both in school and in my career, God has shown up when I needed Him. I always had to do my part, but in cases where that was not enough, God stepped in and more than made up the difference.

I encourage you to invite God into all aspects of your life. He can make you better at everything you do, and as you learn to rely on Him, you will find that His presence and aid becomes a source of supernatural peace.

Are there areas of your life where you have shut God out? Open up and invite Him in, and see the difference He will make.

Stepping-Stones

- Take some time to pray about the struggles in your life. If it is important to you, it is important to God.

- When you pray, thank God that He is bigger than your problems. Acknowledge that you don't have any issue in your life that is too big for Him to handle.

- As problems (new or old) come up, reflect on the joy that you don't have to face life's challenges alone.

Signpost: *Challenges build us up.*

Good Gifts

Hasn't this rain been wonderful? It was so desperately needed, as we are in the midst of a serious drought. And isn't it remarkable that we only average a little over two inches of rain the entire month of January, yet we got almost twice that in only a matter of days?

I truly believe this was a gift from God, and God only gives good gifts. But wait, you say. What about all the people and businesses that had leaky roofs and water damage? What about all the car accidents on the slick roads?

I also believe that gifts can come at a price. Think about what you got your kids or loved ones for Christmas. For many of us, buying those gifts involved saving up for them and sacrificing other things so we could buy those good, perfect gifts. But ultimately, they were worth it.

Think about the trials you have been through. They are never fun and are often really hard, but at the end, the gift we receive is stronger faith, deeper trust, more patience, or a better understanding of who God is. Ultimately, those are all good gifts.

Matthew 7:11 says, "If you, then, though you are evil, know how to give good gifts to your children, how much more will your Father in heaven give good gifts to those who ask him!" (NIV). If you ask Him for patience, He's not going to just give it to you. He's going to bring situations into your life so that you can learn patience. If you ask Him to show you how to trust Him more,

He might ask you to do things outside your comfort zone in order to build that trust. But in the end, it will be for the good. God only wants the best for us, and He has all sorts of ways to accomplish that.

And before you start thinking that sometimes it's just too difficult to endure a hardship to attain the prize, remember the best gift we have ever been given: Jesus's sacrifice on the cross so we might have salvation. Even Jesus had a hard time with that, yet He endured for the greater good.

The next time you receive a gift, or find yourself in the midst of a trial where God is trying to teach you something, remember Jesus's sacrifice and thank Him for His good and perfect gift.

In our world of easy credit and instant gratification, it is easy to fall into the belief that all struggle and pain is wrong. This leads us to the idea that any resistance means, "God just isn't in this." The moment the journey gets tough, we doubt the validity of the journey.

But struggle is part of human existence, and truth be told, we need it. Without struggle, we can find no purpose, and without purpose, there is no peace. It is only as we work toward something that we are able to find contentment. If you have ever been on a really long vacation, there comes a point when it is time to go home.

So don't wish for an easy life. Rather, work toward a fulfilling one. Reach outside yourself, and help others. Most importantly, you need to ensure that your life is right with God, through Jesus's sacrifice, and let Him give you your true purpose and thus your roadmap to real peace.

Stepping-Stones
- Make a list of all the times God has come through for you. Then use that list to bolster your faith and trust when things get difficult.

- Make a list of scriptures that communicate God's love for you. This will help you embrace the truth that He wants what is best for you. Here are a few to get you started.
    - Ephesians 2:4–5
    - John 3:16
    - John 13:34
    - Matthew 7:11

Signpost: Would you run a gasoline engine on water? So why do you try to run your life without God?

Plug In and Recharge

In our life group, we have been studying the Holy Spirit. One of the teachings talked about when we don't rely on the power of the Holy Spirit, it is like unplugging the battery from a smoke detector. It looks the same from the outside, but it is not able to do what it was designed to do. In his book *Mere Christianity*, C. S. Lewis said, "God designed the human machine to run on Himself. He Himself is the fuel our spirits were designed to burn." So if we are not tuning in to the power of the One who dwells inside us, we are like a gas-powered car trying to run on water. Funny thing is, it takes only a little water in a gas tank to really mess up the car's ability to function as designed. That holds true with us. If we begin to think that we are in any way capable of living the true Christian life on anything other than the power of God, we are deceiving ourselves and will mess up living the way we should.

I remember hearing someone say, "When I try I fail, when I trust He succeeds." I love that. It shows that while it is He who succeeds, we are still involved in the process. We need to trust. But first, we need to decide to trust, and once we make that decision, He will give us the power to live it out. We need to decide not to gossip, and He will give us the power to control our tongues. We need to decide not to react in anger—and I don't mean just stuff it down but rather "take the thought captive" (2 Corinthians 10:5) and *choose* to submit to God and allow Him to give us the power to love those the world says we should hate.

I have heard the power of the Holy Spirit described in this manner. Being connected to the power of the Holy Spirit is like stopping your car with power brakes. When you want to stop your car, you have to decide to put your foot on the break, but it is the power of the braking mechanism that actually stops your car. To do it on your own, you would have to be like Fred Flintstone and that likely wouldn't turn out too well. This analogy provides a wonderful view of the Christian life. If you were to open your door and drag your foot to stop your car (rather than using the brakes), you would be about as successful in stopping your car as you will be in living properly through relying on your own power.

As with everything in our lives, living the Christian life is a cooperative undertaking with God. But our part is very much the minor role. I'm not saying it is easy, but it is minor—we need only to submit, trust, set our very self aside, and say, "Not my will, but Your will be done." Much easier said than done (at least for me, but that's just because I am proud, stubborn, and more than a little stupid! And I don't think I'm all by myself in that regard.).

> Submit yourselves, then, to God. Resist the devil, and he will flee from you. (James 4:7 NIV)

Submission is rather a dirty word in our society today. Most likely because it has been grossly misused in the past. But in that word lays the secret to our struggles. Oh, it is not a secret that removes all the struggle from our lives, but rather it connects us to the power that can get us through those struggles. It is important to remember, though, that the goal is to connect with God and build a relationship that allows us to trust Him completely. That trust allows us to submit to His will and thereby get us through the struggles and trials in our lives. Those trials will not stop this side of heaven, so if your goal is to achieve a struggle-free life through a relationship with Jesus, you will ultimately believe that either you or He has failed. Life after all is a struggle, but it is through those struggles that we grow. And if we let them, our trust in God and our relationship with Jesus deepens and strengthens.

Stepping-Stones

- Where are you struggling in your life? Make a concentrated effort to trust instead. Remember that if you have done what is possible, the remainder lies with God.

- Where are you refusing to give up control? Relax in the knowledge that you are loved and give up your illusion of control.

Signpost: True peace and rest are found only in close relationship with God.

Where Do You Turn?

The other day, I had had a bad day. After weeks of pressure from all sides, I descended into what could best be described as a pity party. Why was I trying so hard at work when the rewards of my labor seemed still so far away? Why was I breaking my back for clients just to have other clients snipe at me when things were not moving as quickly as they would like? Was this great big gamble (which God has made abundantly clear is where he wants me) of trying to run a company with just four people really worth it? Why was I still trying so hard when success still seemed so far away? Now don't get me wrong. God has worked countless miracles, and things have improved dramatically over the past nine years or so. But the end game still seems out of sight.

I was tired, depressed, and sulky, and there was very little that was going to cheer me up. So when I came home, I did what any good Christian would do: I turned to the Internet to relax and shut down my brain. After all, why would I turn to the Bible? It's not like the scriptures say, "Those who wait upon the Lord will renew their strength" (Isaiah 40:31 KJV). Oh wait. They do say that, don't they? Well, it isn't like spending time with God has any direct benefit on our physical world with all its strife and struggling. If it did have any effect, there would be a scripture that states something like "Seek ye first the kingdom of God and His righteousness, and all these things will be added unto you" (Matthew 6:33 KJV). Oh yeah. It does say that.

So knowing all this, I naturally began reading my Bible, right? No, I didn't. I logged-in to Twitter, thinking that maybe I'd find a joke to lift my spirits. You know, the wonderful thing about the grace of God is that it meets you where you are. As I perused my Twitter feed, I read the following:

Lee Strobel: "'My sin is to fear what never will be.' - Puritan prayer."

And then …

Rick Warren: "Don't worry, worship!"

And finally …

Rick Warren: "Peace is quiet certainty that God is in control."

I smiled as these all popped up on my screen. I got the definite feeling that God was trying to tell me something. But I wasn't exactly sure what. Okay, I'm kidding; even I couldn't miss this. So I prayed and thanked God for the encouragement, but I wasn't all that encouraged. I mean, I know that God is in control, but how do I know if I am doing everything I'm supposed to do? I mean I (actually Sandy and I) have worked so hard at the company, and sometimes it seems like there is no point. So although I did not turn to the Bible immediately, I did eventually and read the following scripture: "But I said, 'I have labored in vain; I have spent my strength for nothing at all. Yet what is due me is in the Lord's hand, and my reward is with my God'" (Isaiah 49:4 NIV).

Okay, that got me. The first two lines were exactly what I had been feeling and the last two were quite obviously another message from God telling me that He has things under control.

Stepping-Stones
- When you are stressed, where do you turn for comfort?
  - If you already turn to the Bible and to prayer, that is great. Keep doing it.
  - If you turn to other things, do this: for the next two weeks, pray and read your Bible when you need comfort.

- Are you worried about anything? Give it to God, pray about it, and then rest in the knowledge that His timing is perfect.

Signpost: You can't trust someone you don't know.

A Slow Progression in Trust

We don't have kids, and as a result, God has to find other ways to illustrate His patience and grace and just how stupid I can be sometimes. What follows is a short description of just such a lesson.

We do, however, have cats. Our boy cat, Thunder, had some nasty sores on his head and had been suffering with them for a while. We had taken him to the vet and tried various things, but they just weren't getting any better. So we decided that one more trip to the vet was necessary. (We didn't ask Thunder his opinion on the matter.)

I got out the cat carrier and chased Thunder out from under our bed. (How do they know, anyway?) I fought to get him into the carrier and took him for a car ride. (Not the exciting thing for a cat as it is for a dog.) We ended up at the vet and after some discussion came up with a treatment that would work. So Thunder got his shot, went back into the cage, back into the car, and came home.

Now the treatment worked so well that by the next morning the swelling had gone down and the area looked much healthier. And my little boy cat was happily purring as I petted him. It was at this point that God whispered in my ear, "That's what you are like, you know."

And He is right. I will kick, struggle, whine, protest, and yell when He is trying to take me somewhere I don't want to go. And along the way, when things poke and prod me the way the vet tech poked and prodded Thunder, I'll squawk in protest and run back to my safe haven (in Thunder's case, the cat carrier) to avoid the work that is being done on me.

You would think that I would learn to trust my master in the same way I continue to hope in vain that Thunder will realize that I always have his best interests at heart. If Thunder would just relax and let me act upon his life in the manner that is best for him, he would have a much easier existence. Hmmm, I wonder if there is a lesson there.

But just as my cats are far too stupid to learn to trust me, I fear that it will take my lifetime (and maybe my life) before I come to trust my Master completely. But I'm getting there, slowly, one little faith-filled step at a time.

Trust is so important. When we drive over a bridge, we trust those who had designed and built it. We likely don't even consciously think about it—and that is the goal. We need to trust God in the same way. We need to have an understanding of His character that is so clear and so much a part of us that trust in Him naturally pervades our every thought and action. As a small child, I would fall asleep in the backseat of the car because I knew that my dad would get me home, and if there were any problems, he would deal with them. Why did I have this level of trust? Because I had a relationship with him that was so deep that I had complete trust in him. Now if I could trust a finite, flawed human being at that level, how much more should I trust my heavenly Father, who is neither finite nor flawed? Begin today to deepen your relationship with Jesus. As you do, your trust in Him will also deepen.

"Trust in the Lord with all your heart, and lean not on your own understanding" (Proverbs 3:5 NKJV).

Stepping-Stones
- Use the list you made four days ago. Be sure you have included items you might have otherwise written off to "fate" or "coincidence."

- When you encounter new challenges in life, refer to that list. When you are able to discern a pattern of God's help, it will give you a firm foundation upon which to increase your trust in Him.

- When you don't get the answer you want, remember that God has a plan for you, and while He promises it is a good plan, there are no guarantees that it will line up with what you want in a given situation. So you need to make an effort to not allow things like that to erode your trust.

Signpost: Don't rest on your laurels. Use the knowledge to help other people and to deepen your walk with God.

Keep Learning

I am in the process of studying for my personal training certification. I have to read two books that are each at least an inch thick that cover a dizzying array of topics. Just getting through the reading is daunting, to say the least. How much information can I absorb just reading the books versus writing notes, answering questions, memorizing important formulas, using flashcards, and practicing what I learn (i.e., performing fitness tests, identifying muscles, etc.)? If I don't set aside a regular study time, it's very easy to just forget about it or let it slide to do something (I deem) more important.

It's the same with the Bible. Reading it is good, of course, but if you don't think about what you read, make notes about what God is telling you, record the truths He is teaching you, memorize key scripture verses that are important to you, practice, and then apply what you've read to your life, you are just reading a book. Very little is absorbed by reading. And if I don't read and meditate on scripture regularly, I will drift from God. I won't feel His peace, protection, or guidance, and my life will be a lot harder than it needs to be.

If I just read my personal training manuals once through and then write the test, I will fail; a waste of time and money. If I just read the Bible and don't spend time studying it, I am failing God and myself. I learn very little or what I do learn is quickly forgotten because I never wrote it down and meditated on it. It's like the parable of the farmer scattering seed: "Some fell on stony places, where they did not have much earth; and they immediately sprang up because they had no depth of earth. But when the sun was up they were scorched, and because they had no root they withered away" (Matthew 13:5–6 KJV).

At the end of my days, when I finally get to meet Jesus face-to-face, I want to hear Him say, "Well done, good and faithful servant. Enter into the joy of your Lord." I'd even be happy to hear, "You tried many times and failed some of those times, but you never stopped trying." I don't want to hear, "I never knew you" (Matthew 7:21–23 NLT).

Is it hard and time-consuming? Sure, if you don't have your priorities straight. God should always be a priority. Put God first and everything else falls into place. Once I write my PT test, it doesn't stop there. I have to keep learning and recertifying every two years. Just because you've read through the Bible and have attended a few Bible studies doesn't mean you're finished. You don't know it all. There is always something new to learn. I can't count the number of times that I've read a verse or heard a teaching on it and an entirely new meaning was revealed to me. I may have understood the verse at a high level, but each time I study it, I find a deeper and deeper meaning.

Don't stop growing in Christ and learning His ways. Apply those principles and wisdom in your everyday life. Just as we don't want our brains to stagnate as we age, we don't want our spirits to stagnate either.

For most people, it is fun to learn new things. We get bored in the absence of something new in our lives. So why not combine your love of learning with your Bible-reading time? Dig into what you read by finding a resource that teaches you how to study or begin a Bible-study curriculum (on your own if you have to). You will find it rewarding, as it will become relevant in your daily life. If you don't know how to start, pray about it. If you want some practical advice on starting, read Proverbs. (They are like little sound bytes of wisdom). But as you read, take time to reflect. Ask how they apply to your life. (They won't all apply, but some will.) Don't just read them quickly and check them off. The idea is to get to know God by reading and studying His Word. The relationship, not the reading—that is the goal.

Stepping-Stones
- Read
    - For the next month, read a chapter from the book of Proverbs each day.

- Request
    - Pray before you read, asking the Holy Spirit to reveal the truths of scripture to you.

- Report
    - Take notes as you read.

- Research
    - Search out related themes and scriptures elsewhere in the Bible.

Signpost: *We are called to love the lost and extend grace to our fellow Christians.*

What Is Grace?

It seems that over the past two weeks, everywhere I turn I have bumped into teachings on grace, whether from the pulpit (*pulpits* actually), on the radio, and random conversations with people at the back of the church. The message has been coming over and over again.

Grace, of course, is defined as unmerited favor, the implication being that something bad has been done and not only has mercy (not getting what one deserves) been dispensed, but it has also been followed by reconciliation, or favor, which one also does not deserve given the circumstances.

However, I have noticed that Christians will often use the word *grace* when describing their actions towards non-Christians. In fact, right behavior toward non-Christians is not grace; it is simply love. If we were to say we were extending grace to non-Christians, that would imply they have done something for which we would have the right to punish them—and because we are not allowed to judge them, we can't make that call. So rather than our looking at it as if they have done something wrong and we are simply being gracious, realize that we are simply called to not judge them.

So the logical conclusion is that the only people to whom we can show grace are our fellow Christians. They live by the same code of conduct that we do, and as such, we can identify when they do things that are wrong. (That is dangerous, of course. See Jesus's words about having a "plank" in your eye in Matthew 17.) Thus, we could dispense both mercy and unmerited favor in that case.

I heard once, "Christianity would be a great religion if it were not for all the Christians." Sadly, that is really true because Christians are human and humans are flawed. In any relationship, grace is the single most important aspect. People are hard to get along with (just ask Sandy), but when we truly catch a glimpse of the depth of depravity we have been forgiven, it makes it much easier to forgive those around us. As is almost always the case, it is pride (the belief that we aren't all that bad) that gets in the way of our doing the right thing and extending grace to those around us.

Don't let Satan gain a foothold in your life. Behave biblically and forgive abundantly, extending the same measure of grace to your brothers and sisters as you wish to receive from God, for He says that is the level of grace you will receive. That parable in Matthew 18:21–35 is positively bone-chilling.

While you are actively extending grace to your fellow Christians, be sure to also be treating non-Christians with love and kindness. Sadly, much damage has been done to our witness through the actions of unloving, judgmental Christians toward the lost. They need our love or, more correctly, our reflection of Christ's love toward them. We have not been called to judge the world; in fact; we have been expressly told not to.

Stepping-Stones
- What will change in your life if you begin living more focused on grace and love?

- In what areas of your life do you need a greater focus on God's grace and love?

Signpost: *It is our job to ask.*

Are You Sick?

> Is anyone among you sick? Let them call the elders of the church to pray over them and anoint them with oil in the name of the Lord. (James 5:14 NIV)

So are you sick? Do you need physical healing? What does this verse say to do? Have you done it? How is that working out for you?

Sometimes healing is a matter of faith, and sometimes it is a matter of obedience. God does not promise to heal everything, and we know that not every request we bring to Him in prayer gets answered the way we want. But we are told to bring our petitions to him (Philippians 4:6) and to ask even for our "daily bread" (Matthew 6:9–13). So while it is well and good to pray for wisdom (James 1:5) and a hunger and thirst for God (Matthew 5:6), it is important to remember that we have been told to bring our requests to Him. So it is not selfishness to ask for healing; it is obedience.

In the same manner, we are not responsible for a person's choice regarding Jesus. But we are on the hook for our obedience with regard to telling them about Him. So while we are not responsible for God's actions when we ask for healing, we are told to ask and thus are expected to be obedient. We can choose to disobey, and I do that often, but we really must ask, "What is the point of disobeying in this case?"

So what leads you to disobedience? Is it one of the following?

1. Do you think, *It's not that bad. There are others who are worse off than me*? If so, what's the logic here? Do you believe that if God expends His healing energies on you He won't have enough left over to cure someone who really needs it?

2. "I don't want to be a bother. The elders are busy." Really? Do you think there is an elder in any church who would rather do anything than witness a miracle?

3. "I've tried before and nothing has happened." Okay, now that one hits a bit close to home for me. But the leper had to bathe himself seven times to be healed (2 Kings 5), so why would you give up now?

4. "I don't know if I can take having my hopes dashed again." Yeah, I know that one too. And it is often used in conjunction with "God's plan must include my being sick for some greater purpose. After all, Paul didn't get healed." God specifically told Paul to stop praying for his healing. If God has told you that, by all means you should stop.

We have no way of knowing if our request for healing will result in our healing, and to honestly make that request of God and have it turned down is heartbreaking. I get that, believe me. Have you seen these things I wear in my ears? But we can't let excuses stand in the way of our obedience to God. It is God's choice to heal or to withhold healing, but it is our choice to obey or disobey.

I don't have all the answers on this topic, but I do know what we are told to do. Even as I write this, I can feel part of me shrinking away from it because I don't know if I can let my hopes get raised again and open myself to receive God's gift of faith in this area. I feel like the man who came to Jesus, saying, "I believe, help my unbelief" (Mark 9:24 ESV). But if you decide not to request prayer, don't make that decision because you think God won't heal you. You have to make that decision knowing that you are being disobedient. I know that sounds harsh. And I know that God will love you anyway. Believe me, I know how hard it is to ask. But don't avoid prayer for healing because you think you are not good enough. (Realistically, none of us are, but we are blessedly forgiven and loved.)

I heard a pastor say one time (regarding God and healing), "If He did it before, He can do it again. If He did it for someone else, He can do it for you. And if he did it somewhere else, He can do it here."

I have many stories on this topic, but one of my favorites is this one. My dad was talking to a fellow one time who related the story of praying for someone for healing. When he went to pray for him, he felt God telling him to dump the whole bottle of oil on the guy's head. So he did. Ordinarily, that would make someone mad, but I think the guy was okay with it because he was healed as a result. (In case that gives anyone ideas, let me say this. Be *sure* God told you. I wear hearing aids, and they would *not* react well to immersion in oil.)

Healing is one of the great mysteries of the Christian faith and is most certainly one of the "hidden things" (Deuteronomy 29:29 NIV). Such belongs entirely to God. But to request healing for ourselves and for others is our responsibility. No, God doesn't need us to pray for Him to heal someone, but He often works within the confines of relationships and desires for us to get to know Him and be built up in our faith. Answered prayer for healing certainly builds our faith, and unanswered prayer for healing requires that we rely on the character of God and our knowledge that He is God. And that strengthens our relationship with Him.

I encourage you to ask boldly of our heavenly Father. The worst thing that can happen is He says no to your request but is pleased with your obedience.

This whole idea of healing can be scary, but Jesus has a message for that too.

> Don't be afraid; just believe. (Mark 5:36b NIV)
>
> Is anyone among you in trouble? Let them pray. Is anyone happy? Let them sing songs of praise. Is anyone among you sick? Let them call the elders of the church to pray over them and anoint them with oil in the name of the Lord. And the prayer offered in faith will make the sick person well; the Lord will raise them up. If they have sinned, they will be forgiven. (James 5:13–15 NIV)

Stepping-Stones
- What holds you back from seeking prayer for healing?
    - Pray about why you are reluctant to ask.

- We know that healing is not a given. We can't "command" God or twist His arm. But our relationship with Him should be close enough that we feel comfortable asking.

- Is there something you are not asking for? Take a step of obedience and ask Him right now.

Signpost: *Our definition of good and fair is based on our understanding of life. God's definition is based on how things actually are.*

What about Him?

Fairness as a general rule of behavior is a good idea. We should be fair. We are called to be just and to love, and so we should also be fair but to use fairness as an excuse, for whining is not a good idea. That type of fairness is really just a way to tell God that we think we are getting a raw deal or that He is doing it wrong … Hmmm, sounds a little arrogant when put that way, doesn't it?

I was reading the book of John over the past couple of weeks. I came to the passage in John 21 starting in verse 15 where Peter kind of gets raked over the coals in response to his denying Jesus three times (at least I'm sure that is how Peter saw it). The section where Jesus asks Peter three times "Do you love me?" seems odd in English, but in the original language, Jesus uses "agape" (an unconditional, complete love) the first two times, and Peter responds with the word *philio* (brotherly love). In a move of grace, Jesus meets Peter where he is and uses "philio" the last time that He asks. Nonetheless, this had to sting Peter a little. Then Jesus takes him aside and basically tells him that he will be executed one day. And Peter's response is to look at John and say, "What about Him?" (John 21:21). Jesus's response is very succinct (again, paraphrasing here): "What's it to you what happens to him?" (John 21:22–23).

I think that is a good lesson to think about. God has plans for us, and they are good plans (Jeremiah 33:3), but they might not be the same as what we might plan for ourselves. (In fact, I think we can pretty much guarantee that they are not.) But God's plan is far better. Someone told me the other day that "God's will" could be defined as "what you would do if you truly knew all the facts." What a great definition and recipe for peace in our lives if we could come to accept that whatever God is doing is part of a larger (and perfect) plan, even when (or perhaps *especially* when) we don't understand it. Remember, "The Lord directs our steps, so why try to understand everything along the way?" (Proverbs 20:24 NLT).

So how do you make it through when the plan is not working out exactly to your liking? Seek out the Author of the plan, and spend time talking to Him. That is what Jesus did in Gethsemane—and although that didn't work out the way He wanted it to, it worked out really well for us. Amen? But even so, that time talking with the Father gave Jesus what He needed to carry out the Father's will. So when things are not going our way and we think life is unfair, we need to take our focus off those around us (and thus not ask, "What about him?"), turn our focus to our heavenly Father, and make the statement, "Not *our* will but *Yours* be done."

"Why?," or more correctly "Why me?," is most often uttered by people. Unfortunately, there is not always a simple answer. But when we realize that God loves us and has it all under control, we can cling to that and take comfort that somehow, in ways that are likely beyond our comprehension, things are unfolding in line with His plan for our lives. When we truly understand that "His ways are above our ways" (Isaiah 55:9), we can begin to have peace in the middle of our circumstances.

Stepping-Stones
- Study Jesus's prayer in Gethsemane, specifically the phrase "Not my will, but yours." Understand that this came from

Jesus's knowledge that, at that moment, the Father had a clearer vision of reality and a better understanding of what needed to happen. It came from a position of trust.

- Next time you are about to ask, "Why me?," instead ask, "What am I to learn from this?" And expect an answer.

Signpost: *Don't let your life pass you by.*

Live in the Present, Learn from the Past, Plan for the Future

As we come to the end of a year, some people will have achieved goals they set for themselves and others (like me) will have failed miserably (yet again). And while it is important to have goals and strive for something, Proverbs 29:18a sums that up by stating, "Where there is no vision, the people perish" (KJV). But something can happen to us when we focus almost exclusively on the goal. The goal grows in our minds as does our desire to achieve it, and the resulting frustration that we have not yet done so works to drown out the joy of the present. This is reflected in Proverbs 13:12a: "Hope deferred makes the heart sick" (NLT).

As Sandy and I work with others to build our business, I find that I have my mind and heart set on the end game. I want to build the company, sell it, and go on to whatever the next step is in my life. But I find that I am focusing so much on the goal that it is affecting how I view my day-to-day life. I am worried that one day I'll "wake up" and ten years will have passed and I'll have missed the joy of living those ten years. The risk, I would imagine, is even greater for those of you with children. But it is large enough for me that I have begun to notice it.

In Target today was a small boy (perhaps three years old) who was not pleased with where his mother was going. Although he did not throw himself to the ground, it was quite obvious, given his attempts to free his hand from his mother's grasp and the horrific sound emanating from his mouth, that he wanted to be doing something or going somewhere else. God sure knows how to paint a picture to get my attention. It took me about two minutes, but finally I apologized to God, as I saw myself in that little boy. I did have the honesty to tell God that while I was sorry, I couldn't promise that I would stop whining. But I would try.

So what is my point? Jesus came that we would have life and have it "more abundantly" (John 10:10b NKJV). So while it is good to plan, have goals, and strive for them, don't let your apparent progress (or lack thereof) toward your future taint your present. Each day is a gift: "[each day] is the day the Lord has made; we will [and you should] rejoice and be glad in it" (Psalm 118:24). Don't let Satan rob you of the joy of today and the current season because your present isn't the future you had hoped for in your past. God has a plan for you and will work out that plan in your life. Don't be like that little boy, yelling and trying to get away from his mother. Rather, understand that God's perspective is different from yours and trust that He that is holding your hand, knows just a *little bit more*, and has a *somewhat different view* of your circumstances than you do. And relax in the safety of knowing that He loves you more than you can even imagine.

> My response is to get down on my knees before the Father, this magnificent Father who parcels out all heaven and earth. I ask him to strengthen you by his Spirit—not a brute strength but a glorious inner strength—that Christ will live in you as you open the door and invite him in. And I ask him that with both feet planted firmly on love, you'll be able to take in with all followers of Jesus the extravagant dimensions of Christ's love. Reach out and experience the breadth! Test its length! Plumb the depths! Rise to the heights! Live full lives, full in the fullness of

God. God can do anything, you know—far more than you could ever imagine or guess or request in your wildest dreams! He does it not by pushing us around but by working within us, his Spirit deeply and gently within us. (Ephesians 3:15–21 MSG)

Trust is a very difficult goal to achieve. It is most easily achieved when we are in a situation where we understand our deficiency and accept that the one in control is an expert. Those of us who have no fear of flying would see just such a case when we step onto an airplane. As I have no idea how to fly a plane, I have no option but to trust the pilot. And I do.

Why then is trusting God so hard? Do I think that He is ill equipped to handle the issues in my life? No, of course not. I know that He is perfectly capable.

If I am honest, it is because I am afraid that if I relinquish control (note the irony of that statement), He will do something in a different manner from the way in which I want it done.

So my issue is with trust. Put simply, I am afraid that God won't do what I want. Well, truth be told, no one in my life (including me) always does what I want in the manner that I want it done. The difference with God doing it is that He will always do the right thing and what is best for me (whether or not I want that at that particular moment). The fact is, if I truly understood and believed that, trusting Him would be easy.

God is good. We can trust Him. So let's agree to start, shall we?

Stepping-Stones

- God's plan for your life is way beyond your wildest dreams. Take some time to ask Him what it is, and ask Him to guide you along the path He has set out before you.

- A life under your control will never be the abundant life that Jesus promises. Pray to give up control and ask for the faith to follow Jesus and to live out His will for your life.

Signpost: God speaks to us if we are willing to listen.

Hearing His Voice

While in Winnipeg last week, we visited our "vacation" church, the one we go to whenever we visit home. We were both feeling rather beat down, as Glenn and I had each worked more than twenty hours in four days. Yep, on vacation.

When we were trying to build our company and times were lean, we often joked that we'd love to be crazy busy, as that would be a high-class headache. Well, when you're in the midst of it, it just seems to be a headache, period. Glenn commented that it just wasn't worth it. We were in Winnipeg to visit our families and aging parents and were working way too much. So in church, God was gracious and spoke directly to Glenn through the pastor when he said, "You might be saying to yourself, 'It's just not worth it,' but I'm telling you to stand firm." I looked at Glenn and grinned like an idiot. He was both thrilled to have a direct word from God, but also a little upset. Standing firm is not the easy way. But God rarely gives us the easy way, does He? However, after thinking about if for a while and marveling that his exact words were echoed back to him from God, Glenn was greatly encouraged.

Ephesians 6 tells us about being strong in the Lord and putting on the full armor of God. Four times we are told to "stand" or "stand firm." We have truth, righteousness, peace, faith, salvation, and the Word of God to get us through anything life throws at us. "If God is for us, who can be against us?" (Romans 8:31). Remember that your fight is not against flesh and blood; it's against spiritual forces of evil (Ephesians 6:12). Are our clients deliberately trying to drive us to a nervous breakdown? Of course not. But Satan is using that to wear us down and make us hate something we used to love. So we are standing firm and moving forward.

But standing firm goes beyond this. Are you firm in your Christian beliefs? Are you apologetic when asked what you believe? Or are you confident in your beliefs and not afraid to show them? We need to be firm in our beliefs even if it might cost us something valuable.

We were promised that in this world we would have challenges, be attacked, and feel beaten down and like it just isn't worth it. But we have a source of strength that is without limit. We know that in His strength we can stand firm against any attack of the enemy because, as Jesus so wonderfully stated, "In this world you will have trouble. But take heart! I have overcome the world" (John 16:33 NIV).

Stepping-Stones

- Do you have a decision you are facing?

- What is God trying to tell you?

- Have you asked Him? "If any of you lacks wisdom, you should ask God, who gives generously to all without finding fault and it will be given to you" (James 1:5 NIV).

- Sometimes it can be hard to hear God's voice, and there can be many reasons for that. Here are some steps to help.
    - Are you spending time reading and studying the Bible? Are you spending time praying? The Bible says, "My sheep hear My voice, and I know them, and they follow Me" (John 10:27 NKJV).

But the way you begin to recognize anyone's voice is to spend time listening to that person speak, so you need to be sure to set aside time for prayer, reading, and just being quiet. One word of encouragement: Remember, it is the job of the shepherd to get the message to the sheep. The job of the sheep is to listen.

- Sometimes God's direction is subtle, sometimes it is obvious. But my dad always used to say that it is easier to steer a moving vehicle than a stationary one. So once you have spent time praying about an issue, begin moving in the direction you believe you are to go, and trust (and pray) that God will keep you from going down the wrong path. I have done this many times in my life. God has always faithfully steered me in the direction I was to go.

Signpost: *Focus on what is true, not on how you feel.*

Keep Your Eyes on the Master

We were watching a dog-training show the other day. The dog being trained was always trying to attack the other dogs it passed while being walked. It turned out that it was reacting out of fear and a sense of anxiety. Basically, it was worried about what was going on around it and was scared of the dogs it encountered.

The solution was for the master to watch the dog. When it showed the first signs of being distracted, the master would tug the leash and bring the dog's attention back to the master. The trainer said that the dog had to learn to not pay attention to what its eyes, ears, and nose told it. It was to simply pay attention to its master and process the information regarding its surroundings through the instructions of its master.

See where I am going with this?

We have a prime example in the Bible of someone paying attention to his own senses rather than focusing on his Master.

> "Lord, if it's you," Peter replied, "tell me to come to you on the water." "Come," he said. Then Peter got down out of the boat, walked on the water and came toward Jesus. But when he saw the wind, he was afraid and beginning to sink, cried out, "Lord, save me!" Immediately Jesus reached out his hand and caught him. "You of little faith," he said, "why did you doubt?" (Matthew 14:28–31 NIV)

When Peter interpreted his surroundings through the actions of his Master, and when he kept his focus on Jesus, he was able to walk on the water. But when he became distracted and took his eyes off Jesus, his view of reality reasserted itself and he began to sink.

Have you done that? Have you ever begun something, some endeavor, focused on the Lord? Were so in step with Him that you truly were "praying without ceasing" as we are told in 1 Thessalonians 5:17? Then somewhere along the way, you began to rely on your own abilities, intellect, and understanding. That was when it all began to fall apart.

So what is the remedy? It is simply to keep our focus on the Master and realize that our senses are subject to manipulation. (Ever flinched watching a 3-D movie or an IMAX film?) But our Master sees things as they truly are and guides us in His perfect plan when we keep our focus, attention, and minds on Him. As Isaiah 26:3 states, "You will keep in perfect peace all who trust in you, whose thoughts are fixed on you!" (NLT).

How do you fix your thoughts, your mind, on someone? How do you pay attention to him or her to the exclusion of all else? Well, there are two ways: (1) you choose to do so, and (2) you make your choice easier by talking with them. It is an act of obedience that is supported by prayer. If you are actively talking with God, it is easier to not be distracted by anyone or anything else.

Sounds simple, but we will all fail at some point. The good news is found in Matthew 14:31, where Jesus moved *immediately* to save Peter. And in my studies, I have determined that the "oh ye of little faith" admonition is more of a "Oh, you poor little thing. How long will you struggle with this?" rather than a rebuke.

Think of it as you would catch a toddler just as he or she is about to fall. You know he or she is trying, and you are proud of the attempt. But you are there to ensure that he or she doesn't hurt him- or herself and to set him or her back on his or her feet again so he or she can keep trying.

Two more things to remember. First, Peter checked with Jesus before leaping out of the boat, saying, "Lord if it is you ..." (Matthew 14:28). Second, although Peter got his feet wet, there were eleven other dry men who didn't even try to leave the boat. So if you haven't failed recently, perhaps you haven't been trying anything new for the Lord. Spend some time in prayer to see what plans the Lord has for you. Then take that step of faith. If you get wet, cry out for help and try again. Can't you just see Him smiling at you for even trying?

What do you need to do for God's kingdom? What task has been set before you that remains undone because you are focusing on circumstances rather than on Jesus?

Anxiety and worry come when we view circumstances through our own eyes. Confidence and peace are found when we see things through the eyes of the Master.

Stepping-Stones
- Do you know where God is calling you?

- Are you anxious? Perhaps you are focusing too much on the things of this world or on your feelings. Focus on Jesus.

- Don't be afraid to try. Step out in obedience when you know what you have been called to do. Trust that He will be there for you.

Signpost: Without directions, how can you find your way?

Share His Peace with Others

We just got back from spending a great weekend on the west coast of Canada in a little town called Port Alberni. (We were researching potential retirement spots, but that's quite a few years off from now.) It is nestled in the middle of Vancouver Island off the west coast of the Province of British Columbia. If you asked me for details, I could tell you exactly how to get there, but it is unlikely I would provide you with such information if you didn't ask.

Port Alberni started as a mill town and still suffers from that image. People don't consider it a destination; rather, it is simply between where the vacationers are and where they want to go, a little blip on the highway where you might stop and get some ice cream and fill up your gas tank. But the three million people who drive through it each summer on the way to the west coast of the island barely notice it.

That is unfortunate because Port Alberni has a lot to offer. It has hiking trails, salmon fishing, an old-fashioned steam engine train, bears that routinely come down on the less-inhabited side of the river, boat tours on a beautiful inlet, and seals and sometimes whales show up just off one of the quays right downtown. And yet Port Alberni goes mostly unnoticed. Do you wonder why?

As we were flying out of the Victoria Airport (located three-plus hours from Port Alberni), I looked at the travel brochures on display. The west coast of the island (where people are going when they drive through Port Alberni) had over ten different brochures describing activities from whale watching to zip-line adventures along with full magazines devoted to other spots on the island. Port Alberni had one tri-fold brochure that mostly talked about salmon fishing. I guess it's not really a secret as to why more people don't go there, eh?

I know of another place most people don't go—and for the same reason: the road to get there is narrow and only a few find it. But the road to another, more popular (but considerably less fun) destination is broad and many find that one. Funny thing is the reason most people don't find the narrow road is that too many of us don't bother to tell them how to get there unless they ask (and even then we might mess up the directions).

We read a great book in our small group called *How to Pray for Lost Loved Ones* by Dutch Sheets, and we decided to pray for thirty people we knew (one per day each month) so they would find the narrow road. It is my shame to admit that I don't even know where that list is (and I need to find it). If we were truly, painfully aware of where that broad road leads, we would be building roadblocks, hanging detour signs, and taking every opportunity to point out the narrow road.

There is nothing more important. Commit to making a list of the lost in your life and pray for them consistently and fervently. Get motivated by allowing yourself to fully comprehend where they are going. (You can't think on that particular item all the time, though, or you'd become a basket case.) Pray that they will find Jesus and that He will make Himself real to them. That is how my family found the narrow road. No one knocked on the door. No one, that is, except Jesus.

Jesus went through all the towns and villages, teaching in their synagogues, proclaiming the good news of the kingdom and healing every disease and sickness. When he saw the crowds, he had compassion on them, because they were harassed and helpless, like sheep without a shepherd. Then he said to his disciples, "The harvest is plentiful but the workers are few. Ask the Lord of the harvest, therefore, to send out workers into his harvest field." (Matthew 9:35–38 NIV)

The thing is, if you are working to tell people about Jesus, you know you will be perfectly lined up with the will of God. That idea should give you immeasurable peace.

Stepping-Stones
- Make an effort to display Jesus to those around you. It has become a cliché, but truly ask yourself what Jesus would do as you encounter stresses and challenges in your life.

- Prepare yourself to tell people about Jesus.
    - Put into words (literally write it down) what Jesus has done for you.
    - Make notes on what the Bible says about salvation and how to share your faith. The Billy Graham website at billygraham.org/grow-your-faith/how-to-share-your-faith/tools/ is a great resource.

- Pray for opportunities to share the love of Jesus with others.

Some Parting Words

When I was a child, we used to say, "God loves you and I love you and that's the way it should be." Those words are true for you today. You are loved, and when you really know and accept that, it will change your life.

You were placed on this earth by a loving heavenly Father, one who wants you to live in a relationship with Him. One who wants you to live your life in His presence, filled with supernatural peace and joy. He provided a way for that to happen. Before the foundation of the world, God knew that He would have to sacrifice Himself to restore the relationship between Him and humanity that was broken by human actions in the garden of Eden. It is our hope that this book has either improved your relationship with your heavenly Father or has brought you to the point where you want to have a relationship with Him.

In this book, you have read about walking the pathway to peace, and we have stressed that a personal relationship and reliance on Jesus Christ is a necessary part of that path. If you would like to have that relationship with Jesus, and the assurance of spending eternity in His presence, I would invite you to pray a prayer like the following: "Jesus, I know I am a sinner, and I ask for Your forgiveness. I believe You died for my sins and rose from the dead. I trust and follow You as my Lord and Savior. Guide my life, and help me to do Your will. In Your name, amen."

If you have questions before you doing that, I would suggest you visit peacewithgod.net/ to get more insight into God's love for you.

If you have decided to follow Jesus, we encourage you to seek out a Bible-believing church and begin to live your life as a brother or sister in Jesus. Welcome to the family!

Regardless of your decision, I hope that the words in this book have convinced you of the truth that you are loved and that there is an alternative to the hectic life you have been living. A life of peace and joy is possible, and God is waiting for you to reach out to Him.

Now that you have made it through this book, remember that your journey is not over. We encourage you to continue in the habit of daily prayer and Bible reading. It would be a good idea to find another devotional book or get a Bible-reading plan and be consistent in spending time with God.

Go in peace. We love you and wish you well.

CPSIA information can be obtained
at www.ICGtesting.com
Printed in the USA
LVHW012158080219
606962LV00001B/1/P